DEN OF INEQUITY
THE REIGN OF SVENGALI

FAYE PAPA SEYNI

Ere long we shall be an irrelevant thing of the past; whilst serious signs straw in the wind suggest an ongoing decline of the existence. We dangerously skip positive ethos then negatively crossed the line. The negative fogging the positive at a snail's pace. Be argus-eyed then witness the bizarre harbingers in abeyance. The people walking blind into an ebbing world, then easily misled by constant crock of shit. Fooled by preconceived ideas, they rebel versus the divine tidings, while the Supreme-being is stating every day with serious divine presage as relic.

The world into welter; each coming day with serious cries of pain tied with pile of anathemas. A subjective criticism that nobody can disregard nowadays. An explicit observance, cuz of negative occurrences that the citizenry is bitterly facing. Each coming day several schisms see the light, tied with some enigmatic struggles and tenets, often unlikely for far-sighted spotters. The humans have been blessed then have gotten a carte blanche to inhabit earth without being accountable. God fearing men are eyeing what the Devine already prefigured coming into sight.

Bewilderingly complex, into a world where the truth ain't plain to make it comprehensible. As he early foreshadowed, human's mental makeup does not come up to standard of this boon. The relevant ain't into several human's conception. No positive upshot about that kinda situation, cuz peeps are mentally shaped. Shaped by an inclement world, while our desipiencies humming harder. People have lost the unity's notion, and then cyann manage a freehand without the negative appears in the long run. Unavoidably disreputable characters ride the wave, and then fatally motioned the world into a hellish balls-up. Discerning persons witnessed iterative and efficient shenanigan. Z manipulated spirit cyann hope; cyann hope till his existance turns in nameless gridlock linked with incapacity to cognize awhile to define this whole muddle. Can't put into perspective the good and evil; whilst unforeseeable events turn in major cause of constant fear and incomprehension. The world is a whole muddle; time for the Old Nick looms ahead then whisked ductile persons, who evidence a fluctuant concepts and a soft spot for the philistinism in total diffidence.

The Svengali mesmerized 'em then completely muddled the positive issue. Kinda initiative was positive in the first lead. Maleficent step that truly blown wide open its dexterity to obscure wandering minds into a world where the Old-nick reigning. Obscured fragile spirits till instilled 'em the havoc's art. The world risks a hazardous implosion.

Acquisitiveness turned as major cause of iterative upheavals, everywhere social ills, busts-up and shenanigans arose by acquisitive minds. Positive use was the Devine's goal, pertaining bout the Maker then to have ripeness, when dire straits appear. That step was the herald of a new age. Kinda relevance been strictly blurted to achieve efficiently the spiritual struggle; struggle versus the non-positive enterprise of Old Nick's clique. An enemy clan that widely blown wide open its purpose and sigil's. Into that hopeless odds,

The Supreme Being ingeniously evidenced the crucial demeanor bout to mark off genuineness from an incessant negative effervescence, instead-of lingering about over small-scale things.

During this time, human's mental makeup is sadly evincing unconsciously its inability to make out the genuine purpose of kinda tidings. Bearer of the tidings ain't mouthed negative tidings, just would-like to mature then prod our heed through the hardly reachable and genuine enterprise. Candor in him, when he heralded the functioning of such prospects.

But peeps were sinking into a serious nescience and few of 'em could put it into perspective. Be beholden toward each other was one of the tidings' element, and could limit himself on God's behest only. Chiefly the intimation aimed at that we be genuine god-fearing; even have sometimes the blast comes into us, to take us one meter toward the Svengali. A genuine step to face complexities of a changing world. But it's too late Old-Nick's shadow fogged everything and everywhere. Humans banter the book for a so called distraction, but consigned to oblivion every move without god's agreement is doomed to fail.

Despite kinda guidance, none human being was constrained to foster God's instructions. A sent tidings far from mandatory, the Supreme Being freed humans to be the only head in that dimension. We have the scope free to manage every step our spirit hints at, but later a foreshadowed confession will unavoidably come into light. So you better clean your dirty deeds, before the angel knocks at door.

God has proven to us that he wants beholding our success, and always wants that to happen. Away from reclusiveness is God's instructions that several drongo minds guessed by deep misconception. They have no gumption in their poor minds. Most people have not reluctant shrugging-off God's prohibitions. Won't have any of it turned as genuine definition of such mien, a serious lack of mother-wit then impelled em to assume the nit-witted air. Fear to encounter liberty loss deeply affected their poor conception, till espouse God's predilections is projected as a freedom lost. Several humans being became brutish, since they took their self reliance from Z_GREAT ONE.

A serious lack of perusal, but perpetually evidence aftermaths that thrown the world through a negative cycle. Wretched, crestfallen most of em are, as though we are starting to live in borrow time, "that is nothing other than this world at risk, an unrecognizable world with a serious piles of anathemas. This ain't really quite by chance.

During such mayhem, clan of wise peeps who contend, and penned versus half-wits and clan of brainy mafia makes out that most of em have cliquey. Cuz they stepped into the chamber 666 then got as avocation to foment right and left, by hook or by crook. Get these dorky minds away from kinda turpitude, only God ablest. Only God is able to figure-out what lured these nuts to have an alliance with the Svengali, who will leave these oafs in the lurch. Brainy mafia is really gifted to bamboozle an eejit, a facile manipulation, cuz saw in 'em childish appreciation in all topical subjects.

The citizenry sadly walking blind. Walking blind as dead men walking, at bayed, cuz of chronic lack of ad-rem projection.

Brainy mafia proceeds with specious gimmick, their status drives 'em through another dimension to catch peeps' eyes and confidence's then throw 'em easily into a dark hole with no return, as if they were dealing with bunch of nincompoops. Bewilderingly complex is their vibration; but eases most of their deeds till there is nothing to it, cuz have gotten a negative induction from Z- Svengali.

Peeps with none adventure or with interminable aspirations turned as major sitting-duck of such manipulation. Despite all pledges, it seems that the brainy mafia ain't suited withstanding ethics' crisis, till they renege their assurances. Kinda promises sound monkey business, cuz the thing is haziness. Kinda behavior occasioned conduct disorders, cuz haven't fulfilled affirmations. Not a quite job is that initiative, that peeps fiercely believed its easiness by efficient soft lies. They conjectured, they were committing white lies; but later mutinies notify 'em they were wrong. Most world burghers are no longer law-abiding citizen, then have personality disorder, to be donnish ain't required to construe the genuine core of such observance.

Inexpressible it will be "the world" If peeps were noiseless, then to look people's air; most of us will have their place in cuckoo's nest. Social phenomenon that comes from chronic despair. Peeps are cloyed, cuz negativity became clichéd. Things are achieved in sackcloth and ashes. Overtime each swayer split-hair instead of peruse top-priority records.

Most of rulers turn a blind eye to peeps' suffering, cuz they close their minds to mercy and the human values. Never consign to oblivion, most of em only have eyes on their terminable business. Terminable and no eternal stance. Only God keeps back the everlasting things, a pertinent observance that they all have an authentic illustration. Consigning to oblivion that only God is ablest, and then puts them in such luring stance. Glad the Old-Nick is, cuz succeeded to live down 'bout God in peoples' spirit, easy job in such degradation. So you better shoulda been here venerating the Supreme Being, who made you a notable before peeps' eyes.

Stakes have taken precedence over human life, just an iterative observance. The life of some humans has been shifted down in the last rank, none daze noticed from some peeps. The beautiful creation has been the earth. Why the preterit, cuz stare how most of inglorious shit-stirrers altered it in skid-row and at several spots you peep at. Slum areas have been kicked downstairs in the last rank from gated community areas.

Gated community has been planned out for never being worried by these constant hazardous scenes. By their harmful deeds, they unavoidably thrusted us in the bait of the era 666, and made their first victims to the idiots, who have an imbecilic manner to iron out troubles. Which's nothing other, than the first signs of this unavoidable decline's tokens intricacy. At the same time notified the failure of a generation, and at all levels. Outbreak of violence, felonies of all kinds done by these ratfinks step-up, and nobody can mosey outside nowadays.

Middle-class has cold-feet then does not dare to hobnob the youthfulness. Moneyed peeps fear youthfulness, at the same time shut themselves away in gated community. Minds are in the qui-vive; suspicious sentiment often directed towards the have-nots. We gotta absolutely alter our manner to live, perceptible sentence for peeps who will meet a click someday through the mind, before that is too late. Cuz we're in the process-of serious decline and only deadlock on this side.

Brave out hardships defined as uphill, until most of people are really fucked up emotionally, trying to get an efficient cure, the booze and the ganja appear as efficient solution. But both mingled hazardously create an explosive combination. Explosive cocktail that only the society and the consumer face consequences. Several world citizens are unable to face intricacies of a changing world. That situation is convoluted, and then provoked the decrease of the faith; the faith of some persons toward their creator. Cuz they don't cotton-on why things move negatively at their side.

What to say about these poor bastards who fuck around right and left by desolation, so hard until their minds are in the process of to let up. Lord, please accept the apologize of my chums to qualify the earth babylon, momentous for our impure existence. According jingoist believers, certainly you wait us with crop. We can acquiesce-in according our negative mien. But there are people who always utter that you ain't resentful, also we concurred with great hope linked with constant fear in abeyance.

Our fear is motivated according the unavoidable eschaton for offenders. The pending question is have we exceeded the limits? 'Bout this topic, every man has his insight, and we got mines. As God erected heaven, and the inferno. As most of us pictured, God does not make things by chance, so our motto is all things got breaking point. God can be a lot forgiver, but also very stern sometimes according our frame of mind. The earth is filled of suppositions, but anyone gotta make-out in guesswork, there is a part of verity that can emerge in the long run.

Even a mouth tells bunkums most of time, don't take it without due reflection, cuz you can rue someday. We gotta know sometimes, through blarneys, there are veracities. About kinda veracities, everyone gotta fumble and keep what rapt his grey matter. Cuz this can be profitable for us to study human's nature intricacy. Welcome to world of vexations, precisely babylon'z era. Where Beelzebub and his bunch of lightheaded strive to mislead people, has who they remain little faith and hope.

Wish you a good land, and hope you already inured your mind to bear ordeals, where everything is upside down, mixed as baby food. Where; ups and downs are tied with us, and hard to give a positive flight. Where most of us wanna fatten their pockets, till make a pact with Beelzebub. Land; where fornication is booming, where all kinda eyesores are topical. Land; where people have no time to venerate God's name. Yet God deserves that anybody leans in front of him, according every second that he gives us a breath.

The most fateful is God already tips-off humans to shirk harmful acts. But most of us are mired in numerous blotted files that we can't blot out its contents, the tipping point. We head straight towards pangs of conscience. Pangs of conscience tied with a real blue funk, if God does not use his mercifulness. Several hearts have been terrified, when they ran across death pangs, realized realities they have taken as cock and bull story. The doomsday will be very well-off in high shiver. Kinda meeting can be painful for Beelzebub and his bunch of jackass, according chauvinistic believers. Frightening day, cuz world is turned up in era of pain by villains, and often a Shangri-La for some who rallied with the devil. Observe humans' laws and human's behavior in all its natures. The good step is, do not being lured by their manner to proceed, if it does not law-abiding to God. Cuz the day of reckoning, you can be in cahoots.

Our villainous attitude, our feeblemindedness and our lack of ascendant over forbidden desires will are the ruin of us. Never consign to oblivion that God will crop-up for every dereliction of duty.

Do not relying-on apropos this sentence is a serious wrong end of the stick, shivering day for every soul, a genuine credence thrown us to lick such reflection. God already forewarned, we shall do you, all you did someday, a serious homily, but free to picture it as you weighed. We are not able to deal the divine wrath; just notice an invisible castigation throughout us. As luck would have it, God got an eraser, an eraser for those who deserve to have a sight of it, so pray fiercely to be included in such leniency.

Cuz we shall bow down and begging for it anyway. Most of us consider this maxim as a lark, opposite several people, who go all out sussing God's speeches. Known all utterances from him, are so bonafide as air that we driving to breathe. Ain't a fable is the nether region; peeps who have the blast could not care less. The clan of insousciance can easily notify candor as spiel, but when the hellfire appears; it's late. Most of us will dwell in the pits, if that trend is kept as frame of mind. Mind about it, cuz in all cases, we shall be gaping when this horrendous event before our eyes.

Cuz even if you slip-out by the will of God. You will eye the allied of the prince of darkness getting a harsh castigation. Word of advice from that Great, God has not need of universe. Perspire on your forehead, when the death angel will crop-up to recover what belongs to the Master. During this excruciation, where is the Tempter your so-called buddy? God is patient, cuz all downed deeds will be treated the doomsday.

Without God's rubber we're down the drain everlastingly. If we don't make-up for mistakes that we have done, we head straight toward jahannam. Gallantry will has any more meaning, when the destroying angel before people's eyes. People will blunder about, for an impossible narrow escape. No narrow escape in such dimension of mystery. This will be every man for himself. Awhile selfish persons will recollect to God, reminisce 'bout perpetrated offences will turn as topical, whether good or felled.

A world of dissents, while some folks are struggling, others are collaborating. Odd is the death that constantly throws us into the deep mystery, but the next day peeps consigned to oblivion they put someone into the grave. You will get stranded, only your deeds through the world will take you where you must dwell. A mystery that we cyann master just to remember us the Supreme intelligence above persons: No equivocacy can emerged from such situation: Those who wisecrack today could weep tomorrow; those who are well to do can turn debt ridden tomorrow, and so on.

The human who clings on life, does not cling has nothing. The life will be the first to ignore you, when the death knocks at door, then followed by ungrateful peeps. Into the tomb you will stare empty, the sense of such situation slowly sinks into you. The love is no longer sufficient, cuz nothing has no longer a value. Get a sharp bird's eye of view bout the world that really surrounds you (illness, corruption, derisory idols, materialism, and lack of faith.

A criticism sight evidenced to us several peeps kowtow when petroleum, gold, wampum come into sight, even illicit funds ain't make 'em think twice. Roots are rotted, high level of degradation comes up on the surface, uproot this stinky degradation turned as overriding way outta, overriding for a so called positive upshots in next coming years. We all have a heart, either dark or pure, only your deeds will notify what side you stand. What is sure is the noble souls don't like the injustice. An obvious arrogance to want saving the world.

You can't relieve anything from trouble in this plight; the only issue is to pray and to save yourself in this perverse society, before to join the demon's clan. God always comes in the last moment, when you proved yourself in minor enticements. Don't think that only God is in this world, you need to be mindful; looking the steps you're 'bout to actuate. The human alleged to be lowly, but wanna mastering everything in his route. Who has not the mind which is excited by the glory?

Reaching has no importance in God's conception, and will never take a little part into it, instead of major part of that one. A possess is often destructive then can easily delete a positive conception as virus. Nothing is life, but that one is inscrutable at some levels. As the science seems being inefficient, to give responses about really interesting questions. Keep his self-regard in all events deeply advised, even get stranded. Chaos turned as new law, initiated by manipulators. Follow us in this era, and you will espy a part of these sensible files that keep on to accrue day following day.

But a thing is free from doubt, you will catch a glimpse the value of your self-rule, and your elation, when it gone. Cuz if your wit is taken off things, often you ain't gifted to suss the better for you. The sole asset that we have gotten is we already bitten the sense of right 'bout doomsday. Nobody can tell dunno, cuz omnipresent is internet. When an event happens somewhere in the globe, peeps get each narrative of it instantaneously. No escape about the sheduled confession, god is waiting.

We live in a lost generation, unfaithful generation, blind generation; world population is confronting iterative frustrations. All negative names can be suitable to describe such generation. The worthy and genuine demeanor been neglected; everything is about sex, dupery, outliving and making money. Booty or clean money doesn't matter. Interests took advantage on their common sense; a comfy settee is not everlasting, good fortune can't last. Pretending to be God fearing man, the human being embodies that constant mutation.

The supreme-being been excluded from human's conception. Sign of rebellion which is an exact replication of Old-nick's attitude. To be a genuine god-fearing man requires a genuine stamina linked with no fcikle honesty; do not sink in this den inequity. Living the life as devil's acolytes, the thing became ill-natured; nothing is sacred, while confusion turned as major cause of concern. They really glad, the Old-nick gave them what they really wanna.

They got a liberty for being free as fishes in ocean. But ocean concealed traps, invisible for naked eye, so stand against negative happenings if it appears at your side. Around the world crowds love the old-nick then venerate him unconsciously for daily distraction. He lets them perform their offending game, to appreciate later the negative charm of idiocy. People have no limitation when they step into the ban; they sink very seriously within this worldly. The life became a trap that turned most of people unconscious and blind.

The life became a prison and a serious nigthmare, for some people who perceive their mistakes lately. People have fear of what they early engendered, but it's late, things took worrying appearances. The human's faith diminishes as his values and mores disappear gradually. The jinx, debauchery and difficulties are everywhere, and then spread dangerously. Strange manner to live that seems being one way with no return.

The cowardice is growing, they all turned a blind eye, and they don't dare achieving a step of peace to fight the unfairness. The idea of fairness kills some people's interest. They all stumble into the Old-nick's guile; the unfairness is synonym of the world disorder. How you can think struggling against the violence, if you favour the unfairness? You can dehumanize a human's spirit by violating all his rights; don't be outstanding to see them hand to hand with devil. A constant manipulation initiated by punsters sank the world, and then annihilated last hope that some peeps could have. The unfairness led them, till become accomplice of plots and massive crimes.

So better remain on good terms with leaders and to keep interests before being persona non grata vis-à-vis other countries. The line between love and hatred annihilated; the aversion steps up. So blind, most of them think it's the suitable way to behave. Constant confusion born sinner, without discernment, the failure became inevitable. None positive perception emerged from kinda scrutinize, or really inefficient to get it positive.

The nowadays system is overriding for gifted manipulators; they use silent strategies of diversion. They easily turned the attention of people toward futilities and throw 'em through a constant confusion. Incessant manipulations, they use the distraction as redoubtable weapon; our lives are flooded by insignificant initiatives. That constant mutation is in progress; the human being embodies it. That strategy of diversion is successfully elaborated by an invisible clan, and then puts considerable obstacles to prevent people to cognise awhile. They everyday muddled the issues, when some people smell a rat, when a thinker becomes recalcitrant they silence him.

The system is very hazardous then leads toward a considerable disaster and hate; time that the communitarianism and sects appear. The new slavery is behind that scenery, a general slavery where the colour of skin does not matter deeply, but your rank in the society. The problems of the world are initiated far from prying eyes.

The problems of the world are initiated before the eyes of idiots who are more than the half of world population. The problems of the world are initiated before the eyes of idiots; cuz manipulators know never kinda people will get the picture of soft shenanigans. The problems of the world are initiated away from genuine thinkers who can easily smell a rat. They proceed silently and slowly as snake in the grass. They enforced some destructive laws, behind these laws, are automatically hidden the force of certain lobbies. Step by step they turn the world at their advantage, whilst world citizens launch into other insignificant matters. They reduce the world for that their clique decides about the fate of everyone; a negative strategy that turns the mind of thinkers inefficient and tired, whilst the remaining of world population got their minds turned as wandering spirits. They became dumbbell. They have the soft manner to convince recalcitrant persons, convince them in exposing things as difficult but necessary for blocking a so called hindrance. If there are recalcitrant minds that they can't silence, the payola silences apprehensions.

So they accept the thing with resignation. Most of the world population behave as children, or perceive the development of the world as children. Manipulators perceive in em childish mentality, and then constantly teach them the art of idiocy, the mediocrity and the constant lack of respect toward God. They inculcate them the fear of the other, the ignorance and the distraction too. The people shouted everywhere the differences and the gap between citizens.

These same people who shouted on every housetop, orchestrated indirectly their situation, the gap they talked about they are the instigators of it. They turned you oafs, vulgar persons and uncultured. If you were foxy and vigilant, things will take another direction than worrying appearances that you are facing today. Never the gap of ignorance will be filled, if you had not thought hindering it in the first sight. You are condemned to live in that constant mediocrity. If someday you sussed out, you cyann act against that initiated system, you risk kicking the bucket as hero or being ostracized.

Died as hero but easily consigned to oblivion by common run people. This will be incessant uprisings and repressions without positive results, if you live in police state. They make them believe that the world is hard everywhere, that's right, but even the plight is here what about instigators? You are the cause of your own situation; your insufficiency in several aspects of the life turned your life incomprehensible as negative creature of habit.

The idiots peopled the world; everyday they mistake, kinda people put their lives explicitly in social networks, for hallucinating purposes. The social networks had as purpose to gather people and to exchange positive ideas for better advancing the world. But nowadays polluted by unconscious people came from everywhere in the globe. They put their lives explicitly; even some thinkers dissuade them to behave of kind.

Teens rush into that system without master it. They can't see the perversity and the dangerousness of it, if they use it for another goal.

Countless people are subscribed, because the friends or parents are subscribed too. If you dare unveiling a criticism voice; you are directly ostracized by adepts of social networks. Their ignorance brought several people, adults or teens in some scandals. Often these scandals are irreversible. You can see several settling of accounts, those who wanna avenge then decide to divulge some embarrassing histories and pics on the timeline of adepts. The goal of it is, to deeply destroy the reputation of the victim.

One does not need to inquiry so far to know the life of several people, cuz the social networks ease the work. Images and comments are undeletable, some marriages been shattered because of this lack of conscience toward the harmful effects of some social networks. Predators are really glad, they widely got there what they were looking for.

Potentials victims who are unaware of cyber-delinquency found themselves trapped in some destructive stories, stolen identity or several harmful happenings.

You will be in constant nightmare, if you wanna initiate something positive. The gap turned in huge challenge, when they realized they rubbed the wrong way. Some people dished out some positive steps then testified, but their thoughts been turned aside abruptly by sceptics. They really disturb, cuz they often behave the manner contrary. The Old-Nick notified as the animate being that's been pointed out as the driving force that turned world into welter.

A value judgment, the skeptic persons are used to spit of kind according poignant adventures they early faced. Some of 'em reasoned that he currently urges persons on to be constantly lured by the prohibited mien. "The Supreme Being is here watching then can easily break through the inscrutable". It seems that's not a welter of words, but a genuine sentence that fragile mental-makeup can't perceive in the first glance.

Leafy minds have taken that iffy to specify kinda science as virtual reality. They all gainsay then are tripping on the issue.

We know that some realities have been drawn to keep peeps' minds jejune, and then throw 'em away from the axiom; and others to turn people mature. When we early mouthed in the sentence "we got it" this only involve persons who cast about; figured out then ascertained the incongruity. 2 mutually exclusives sciences, we all eyewitness when they spar.

We kick the immature science out till that becomes nil; there are no flies on prudent persons, and then figured out that the major purpose is to turn fragile peeps cray then noxious. Forbidden pleasures, culprits will respond about, due to their never ceasing execration. You will get busted, when you kick the bucket, cuz crack of doom follows.

The humanity has been reduced in an era of mishaps, and then mixed up with dangerous levels of perversion that evildoers use as traps. What saying about communities that became very sectarian, rotten-hearted and who lack a bit of direction.

The disrelish, the pleasure to outrival the fellow citizen, the pleasure to prejudice and the recurrent thirst to domineer, that's nothing other than a little facet among the dark aspects of human's nature.

Human's aspects that nobody agnize, and can't agnize. It became damn hard to enshrine it in the positive way; if God does not throw a tinge of noesis through foxy spirits. Facets that will take a vague time before the brainy spirits be able licking it, and being brooked by their kinship group.

They all are gaping; the one who used to be in troubles doesn't gape. The normal humans are only watching the negative fogging the positive. Anyway to express about it will append another ply in the incomprehensible behaviors of human being. We shall to risk having white hairs without unravel the closed book and to send it in a positive flight, just trying making out that devilish mental make-up that they anytime feeding. That version of human nature has always been ubiquitous for vigilant minds; of course.

The thing is a disgusting finding for the no vigilant people, and who really are following the virtuous mores in the era of criminal minds. No doubt their souls belong to devil, wise mouths are shouting negatively, but none major positive incident through their minds denudate of grey matter. They keep-on being nuts about Satan. Several persons don't know where the negative wave is on em, but some of 'em really conscious they hold it, then inefficient struggle against. Kinda negative waves can throw us into dark, either knowingly or unconsciously.

Nobody is an angel, stumble into trap is not impossible in everyone's life. The meeting with the word "sin" seems inevitable in modern times for anybody, even the no reliable to suspicion, keep it in mind. Ain't know my dear, if you will be able living in this era and having force on this nerve-racking levels; then keeping on line that revenant emotional disturbance through your spirit. We are living or we are starting to be wolfing into an infernal and no positive spiral.

We are gulping down in that foggy tunnel, hard to apprehend then seems endless; locked down system whilst nowadays junctures turned the future iffy. Several souls plodding on; a spooky message for the future age; your life is delineated as ineffable.

You gotta sweat about that ineluctable coming reality that will be toe up. They try screening that your world will be soon turned in babylone. They jacked all resources then doubled up it; altered rules in mob rule. Peeps will be left in the lurch, when moment appears. Peeps will sell out; cuz they will never push through kinda obscure reality.

The loss of traditional values keeps on its ominous progress. To live ill-advisedly been taken-in and always in conflict with virtuous mores as foxy minds figured out. God strictly forbade it, and linked it with indescribable retribution. Beware of it; cuz the Supreme Being can lose interest in the sentence; when our minds dare going into the negative. Go following world's vices then have a handshake with the Old-Nick, don't yammer when God decides giving you the go-by in the zero hour. Everyone commits sins in his style.

Even if they get all the time to explicate you the Supreme Being in the era that we are living, you certainly risk choosing the progress and vices as others already done. About sins no hope for the future generation, we're unworthy then proceed away from praying eyes. The future generation will proceed in daylight. In that track you will cop the negative, sliding every day in world's vices and troubles. A comportment sanctioned by a divine punishment, according some hearsay.

Entrapped into 666's fog, under a real continnum aspect, you will hardly meet the genuine mind, genuine thinker who will be able to define every aspect of that intricate landscape. He's blinded too. Discernment is visible in vocab's pages, but does not make sense in the society. Discernment the zealots of Satan haint. You cyann get something positive, when the Old the Nick takes out deep nous on your mind. You can easily get every line, if you step into God's area. Inacessible step for people in a bit lack of direction to cotton on primary projection of the discernment.

To take off interferences that turned you deaf then clouded your human's eyes, only God ablest. We don't talk about religion, but only human's cleverness that God infused into his inefficient mind. Inefficient mind that only able puts in perperpective worldly's stuff. Try to put things back in their origin spot, and to leave the freedom from want that turned us in slave of incessant insouciance. God's kingdom is watching to better judge the doomsday.

Only victims don't figure it out yet, we all are victims of something, directly or indirectly. The discernment is no longer sufficient to restrain his mind then to constantly send it in the positive. Responsible of some deeds we are, and consequences this may engender in the long run. No need being jinnee to cotton on and gazing at through mystery, but just to be argus-eyed and striving to tell apart the real from fake. In disarray the world is every day, whilst the peeps ain't fathom how life moves and its current unforeseeable traps.

The Old-nick turned most of us in cavia-cobaya then tragic outgrowth appears everywhere, whilst worst is surfacing everywhere in globe' nooks. In the idea to wait the last hour, we are living in a tragic era, wars break out almost everywhere for some people's interests. Kinda immoral deeds incite big-guns to think that they are the heroic persons in this era. All their plots through the world turn in media event, and are materialized by a so called success, often tainted by indescribable cruelty.

Worst, they even think they are hero of beyond; the only hero is the one who will turn his blue-funk in genuine grin after the meeting with God. Cuz getting positive judgment from the Supreme Being, foxiest between us are dreaming. We are fighting against the sanctimony; hate it then unable to eradicate it, cuz that's a part of us. Everyone between us already used hypocrisy to save or to bring into deep someone that he considers harmful for his upturn. Some persons sacrifice themselves for humanity; a positive go-ahead, when you perceive it from outside, achieving positive deeds for the humanness.

But turn in illegitimate enterprise, when devil himself steps into the enterprise. During they lend a hand, some truants are sporting this fake suit to rig everywhere and everything. They punk people then are using lip-service as redoubtable weapon to fool prying minds. Redoubtable cuz kinda gougers perform in silence; they don't act as benevolence, and then got paid every time that their service been asked; or get illegally dough. They also earn living by that way; they rep nothing.

They are profiting from it, knowing the poverty is an ugly business. Are they ready to eradicate it? The life is wonderful for some people and a real nightmare for others. The life conceals myriad mysteries, beware of it. Nowadays most of us kill each other to have the ugly supremacy, supremacy linked with doubtful files.

They don't know the life is very wonderful, when you stand yourself in the mid. When you amble in some countries peopled or not, you can see its citizens looking each other as noncitizens. Who tells looking each other; think remaining aloof in every aspect, cold reality noticed by mindful peeps.

They all became loco, only negative delirium able gathering them in delirium spots. The compassion only appears when a tragedy comes into sight. And nobody is unpleased, when he sees starved people wandering around. You become disturbing, when you commence to wonder why they don't gather to fight against that dirt. On the contrary most of 'em really laugh, when you mouth kinda issue, and add care about yourself before spit around with kinda archaic ideas.

People are only open about what interesting them, and always get pleased to appear, where their actions will are saluted and mediatized. Hard is to understand, where they found kinda dirt mentality; but God is up on all that. They all wake up a day with a brainwash; or they always hide kinda bestiality into bottom of them.

With all happening through the world nowadays, the dissent spreads. They told judge someone is no good and people really like to judge others. To judge; that's something and to notice facts then relate it; are another issue. Criticize by badness or just to have something to tell is lousy.

They act up and spit criticism statements following matters they got from a talkative mouth. Often linked with a precipitation to act, they run their mouths without investigate deeply the interest of the informer.

Most of us belong to kinda frame of mind, cuz the human being likes monopolize and judge to have eyez on him. The patience doesn't include in his deep desires. His deep desire is to be entirely superior to others; and all the time. Through his eyes you can eye the ferocious adversity.

Through the minds and eyes of immature people, the words noble and generous are hiding something no positive. The noble is a poor human and the generous wants bribe someone, or buy something that he really wants and that he can't afford or the capacity to have in the legal way.

The human's spirit is filled of fantasies; and futilities. Worst is; according other immature souls, the noble wanna turn them fool and avoid showing he is really broke.

This idiot judgment been stated; because they ain't able to read his mind, and to break through the mystery. They really prefer the wealthy, or the high roller who lives beyond his means then get broke before every end of month. Always trying to fool people, show and wear what they can't afford.

My people know some of them are stunna. When disaster comes, we all used to hear they all are same trickster. The noble mind is really hard to hem in; by their discipline and state of mind. Often newsmongers designate them as archaic spirits, cuz they spend no time in futility and throw no buck down the drain.

Attitude pointed out negatively, as if they were looking for something with a malicious skill. Really excited by an evident envy of luxury, the idiots look down on the sober persons. They only contemn 'em, cuz of the lack of action toward wastage. They really disdain the megalomania; you can't affect them; even you spit your malicious gossips all over the place.

As the immature minds don't like the low profile, their weakness incites them to describe deez people as drongo in unfounded way. Through our investigation about the degradation of the common decency; we've noticed a terrible indecorum from people, unbelievable and indescribable behaviors.

These shits seen the light, but we are always unable to understand and to tell, how human being gets involved then slid in kinda scandals. From the Old-Nick's claws some persons got repugnance from their negative deeds, first victory. The sensation to have committed a sin, is a little success to take in consideration 'bout his negative steps.

A feeling that several people haint, so worldly widely in em. The word sin has anymore effect in people's mind then does not hinder their conception. The one who dares telling sin, think directly to forbidden things. Success inside it; kinda sensations propel in genuine discernment, but conceal a deep feeble mindness. The lure of gain became primordial for people's mind, till they forgotten the sense of life and the Supreme Being.

The struggle to earn living became fierce and turns people's mind to become grasping; whilst the lewdness spreads, religious values got annihilated.

The prostitution is changing face, and became attracting. Countless wenches step into kinda squalor; they behave of kind after work to make easy money. They all became greedy; trying to fool detractors, they haven't the same outfit as the professional's. They also embody the degradation of moral decency. Different motives been mouthed; those who are in family's home, who not seem being exposed as those who already left the family's home, no alternative they are obliged to cope every minute etc....

Most of 'em handle the prostitution as lucrative activity to be really in touch with the superfluous, through a consumer society with none moral. The obsession toward the superfluous is not a definite characteristic towards a minority, neither the characteristic towards young citizens of the world. But that's a universal aspiration as an air vent been created. All ages meet together and for all types of motives; a cause of concern for conservatives.

When they about to criticize this alienist mentality; the adverse camp argues that detractors like talk trash toward 'em. In front of this spread of prostitution networks, some protagonists are trying to deny accusations against this illegal activity linked with the prostitution, just to find an honorable way out. This refusal of this reality is really overwhelming, or the libertinage is really their custom. This dirt easy going boosts the pervert minds to launch into the sex tourism. Every year through the world, and more in countries where poverty hits incessantly, rubbernecks go abroad and most of them are portrayed as dangerous perverts.

This societal phenomenon has been worsened by the influence of internet, and the word to mouth. In that muss; several trippers choose their destination according the sexual attraction. In some countries the promiscuous sexual activity is not reprimanded as it could be; cuz that's a means to earn money; whilst governments wait a huge share.

You all eating and make business with booty, these odd vacations have been stimulated by a negative air duct of perversity.

All that mess before the eyes of authorities. Involved authorities have an only preoccupation, the one to attain more overturn and tourists. This shameful trafficking turns in win-win situation for everyone between them.

Kinda persons are ready to prostitute, just to have some buck, to eat and or buying some insignificant stuff. These inglorious persons in a bit of lack of direction are exerting sex domination, cuz they are ruling by wampum before the have-nots' eyes. Unholy manipulation that everyone between them is thinking has a benefit; is nothing other than the first preliminary of the hell on earth.

This dirtiness does not always happen between consenting adults, but spare nobody among people without dignity and virtuous mores. This diabolical behavior reached several minds, even children and babies not spared so. In sadism game is mingled all kinda sadisms and sexual fantasies, sometimes crimes appear. Paedophilia, scatology till the zoophilism; shut my mouth before to be solicited by the lord of flies.

May God has a pity of our souls, I don't know if Satan's clan thrown humans into the dark hole, if the case it is really strong. The insouciance of youth about the shit that spreads through the world can be comprehensible. Those who shoulda show them the way to take have been disconnected from the moral decency; in stepping in squalor every day. Their moral decency has been negated in the first contact of that shit. Sex tourism becomes problematical, cuz lot of people enjoy of it deliberately, even the no liable to suspicion; then became really hard to excise.

These consenting adults are the victims of worst slavery that humanity registered; through a world that they have no more value than the vulgar things of life. They are treated like that, as insignificant humans and often linked with abuses. Kinda abuses often turn in dramatic events; and often mentioned innocent children. The prostitution was often practiced by people who came straight from disadvantaged areas. But nowadays it affected all ages and all sectors of the society; advantaged or disadvantaged area.

These sex actors or actresses are all harmful for the society; even they earn living by their own. The most negative are sexual vagrants who make transactions to relieve their libido, and their thirst of diabolic domination. Behaving of kind; they always think to be the indispensable persons of that dirty game. But in the next step the aids appears at its turn to serve as stern umpire and to send the most libertine minds in the mysterious God's kingdom. All kinda prostitutions see the light; among them the discreet prostitution based on elaborated plans to escape from sanctions.

The only purpose for some between them is to improve their means to earn living and others to slide into the superfluous. With misery in the world and the opening of frontiers, the myth runs all over the place and in the 2 ways; rich or poor countries. Some pimps encourage desperate women to reach their dreams, in going toward countries which are pointed as Eldorado to earn money easily. All these promises are tainted by current lies; lies that the victim will taste the charm later.

All that mess has been provoked by some hasty conclusions and consents without take the time to lick the charm. Casual consents that some parents done most of time, when they hear the words money and success, without get suspicions their daughters will make pact with Beelzebub; one way or another. The sex exports itself and transports itself following the solicitation in a side toward another. The buyer and the seller are all the victims of this system; industry with well definite levels. Levels that you can escalate according the money you got; the charm and what you have as skills.

High end prostitution attracts some businessmen, a kinda prostitution that a broke man can't afford. The fantasies told 'em to have sex with hot scort-girls; they think kinda coition is different of the other. You only pay for the same, but with onerous price. That sentence shows to us that discrimination and egoism are everywhere and the only way to escape from it is to be made of money whatever the manners. But the legal way is deeply advised.

The attracting bosoms or if I dare tell it; those with silicone or attracting booty have a price in that crazy world. And many men pay crazy sum to spend night with kinda women, if they are prostitute. The traffic of women, and dissimulated under the tourism and corruption, revealed to us a globalization with uncontrollable consequences. We often noticed a sordid universe of children who are kidnapped or sold in a point to another of the globe; and often with the consent of parents. The whoredom became a way to earn money and a survival key of that modern era.

We must underline the variability of prostitution's universe; those who prostitute to buy brand new attires and stuff; and those who make it for the surviving struggle. These methods are the fastest ways to accede in prostitution industry. It is so easy to be in prostitution industry; but damn hard to annihilate it, or to get out from it. The best way to eradicate it is to re-educate the people; a damn hard work, cuz most of 'em are already lost forever.

It has been said that every sin is an offence toward the Supreme Being; and all of them mentioned will start our decline. The sin causes direct or indirect consequences in the life of a human being. Without care about it, the sin contributes in their daily difficulties. It becomes dam hard to avoid the sin, cuz the soul of most of people live for kinda attraction, and even they know the harmfulness of it. The good humans of all epoch are those who sow wise ideas in desperation to see it moving positively. They are the guardians of wisdom; but they are seeing their strength decreases, cuz every day the devil spits. When we consider archaic the manner to think of somebody who turns himself aside from futilities, and ephemeral things, this means you're a drongo. Early or later; if your soul sees the light through a positive way, don't you think you will see the life in a different way? The dissents destroying us and define us as ridiculous before the noble souls. The end of a pious man is sad but also wonderful, cuz going in the mysteries land, where God is the only master.

In the past preoccupations about virtuous mores has been noticed in the peoples, code of honor; the shame feeling, all that with the sacred sense of marriage. The importance of the virginity was fundamental in all continents, then structuring durably the relations between men and women. The inherence of that civilization lost all its capacity in worldwide; most of women become prostitute by choice and less by constraint. They are looking for the freedom in that dirty way, cuz the easy money leads and manage their future.

In same time their state of mind propels them toward an indescribable libertinage that allows them to decide as they wanna of their libertine relations. A terrifying insousciance, until they are treated as stars in their families than vulgar victims of that harmful worldly. Unconsciousness based on money, cuz their daughters become offering before their eyes and don't consider themselves as money and sex slaves. The harlotry is stimulated by all kinda persons and the spread of bagnios through the world; so attracted by this world where the sex is buying as scones.

Some predators recommend persons to go in some destinations through the world to have bid price, without forget explaining each narrative of that business. Not hard currency in some countries; and their prostitutes earn small amount of money than prostitutes of rich countries. In these conditions, the tourists of rich countries have no difficulty to select knockout women cuz they become the kings. The sex tourism turns in triviality in worldwide, and not always happens in poor countries, but everywhere in the globe's nooks.

Deliriums, fantasies and indecent vices, people pointed out as responsible; but who are the actors and actresses of these unworthy files. Who are those who imperatively wanna explore the sex of persons from neighbor countries or continents? This is not a quest to avoid the poverty and help most of 'em to out; but only a quest of fantasies and an extreme triviality of that shit. In some countries where the religion is omnipresent are victims of that practice. Illegal practices that nobody can fight; that practice gives people to eat every day.

Try to rub it out, can incite peeps to give you a chase, if you are resolute on that decent way. A visual difference between so-called virtuous lands and profligate lands been noticed; they always got a hide before to launch in dissipation.

That kinda harlotry is practiced in hiding; debauchery that numerous lasses are practicing far from prying eyes; even they got husband or boyfriend, that's their last care if the fella does not have enough dough, or if they really don't love the man. Some men shouted even having a man of substance they can turn gold digger.

They used to be money slave; the money turned some of 'em in irretrievable bawdy wench. An explosive cocktail that blown wide open all its destructive capacity. Kinda anguish appears for insignificant number of persons who struggle all days to put virtuous back into their origin spot.

Since the sex industry boosted with countless benefits, the price of buildings became expensive, and turned in discrimination for have-nots of some countries.

The leaders of some western countries launched into a fight against prostitution of all kinds into their territories, but they straight face a powerful and invisible opponent. Overwhelming number of lasses prostitute themselves everywhere in woods, in pubs, in flats, in sidewalks etc, stopping every passerby and banger that they targeted as easy prey, or to have a string of lovers. Even those who ain't reliable to suspicion floating on that squalor, with provoking attires, most of 'em stroll about to have a trick, gaits that only a man of God can turn aside. A babylone the world is becoming; and subtle hunting technique, you can eye when they about to lay a fatal trap.

A sort of ghetto where neglected fellas or in daily troubles in their couple come to get some relieves. The repression becomes tough until some common women fled the streets. Thinking they definitively wreck the scourge, governments had smile for a so called success; without realized that their early done repression was not efficient; just turned prostitutes in clever.

The repression against street-walkers and pimps turns the situation crazily, for those who fight against em. This situation became complicate; every clan figured out and already planned out another scheme. They policing in plain cloth policeman to get them red-handed; whilst the antagonists turn their evildoings inconspicuous; prostitutes became foxy; cuz got another artifice for working, just to get them desperate.

These hides been spotted in internet platform; massage parlor or in sporting houses, to lead stray every ray and their respective henchmen who are striving to annihilate this praxis. To prostitute on the net became clichéd and simple via meeting sites. This hiding harlotry is terrible and really powerful and spits harmful waves for johns.

Several followers turn around this ungodliness; cuz these females behave as merchandises in shopping mall. All about them are really explicit behind the screen; sizes, measurements; town and celly etc.... A total word picture, then everything gets ready to hire these working girls.

What to say about the "escorting; another form of whoredom, going to accompanying till to get some tail. This is a veiled prostitution which doesn't worth more than the one we already know, even most of them deny. Women and men who prefer named themselves escort-girls or escort-boys just to embellish their immoral activity and do not have the name prostitute; even the practice gives them money most of time.

Nowadays it's normal that files noticed minus groups of prostitutes in the street; even in some countries the business has no time out, and in motion in daylight. But in some countries the business decreases in the streets, because the internet became a primordial refuge for them to perform invisibly and avoid criticisms and penal sanctions.

What about those who define themselves as masseuse and who perform in their apartments and who don't dare seduce passers-by in the streets. The prostitution on the net is more discreet for truants. That is no longer a secret; anybody knows it, even children who became partisans of this squalor.

The prostitution been removed from streets toward internet, even some common women still working in the woods and some specific world streets. A cyber delinquency; with a worldwide propagation, spreads everywhere; the stench of it does not disturb, cuz most of people drown their concerns into it. A sort of platform; where all kinda shits are treated to augment the influence of Satan, unconsciously.

Long time ago that peoples don't wonder about the sense of their coming here; and the sense of life, they thrown kinda subjects in nothingness for decays; unless if you talk about wampum. This aspect of human being is unacceptable and unbearable. The prostitution attracts until attracts the criminals; who get involved of that fruity business.

They emerged criminals industries to have their shares of that profitable pie. They trapped women into zany deliriums, business which has an only dynamic "the money". Kinda criminal industries propelled women in terrible and dark universe and trained them to become nymphomaniac.

They became sex slaves; mistreated and used as affordable merchandises for sex addicts persons. Some women have been forced to prostitute themselves; a terrible and forbidden human traffic. These warnings have never got effect; cuz some persons consider the justice as incapable. A terror built on threats until the confiscation of all means to survive. They all take the risks "the pimps" cuz the business is really fructuous for them.

The prostitution seems being legal in some countries. When some events happen in some countries, governments seem being impotent and having no alternative, they yield for prostitution. Some among them won't create disorder; which can destabilize the good functioning of benefits. In this step most of them hand out sheaths in some towns; where events will be held.

They already foresee that several visitors will not prevent themselves from kinda initiatives. Kinda decision will worsen the apogee of the prostitution in a world of total perdition.

What to say about the diplomatic world which has always strived to reflect a reliable and positive image; an irreproachable image that hides a worrying reality the one of sex and traffic of all kinds. They also enjoy about that; the alcohol; sexy women and all types of perverse games; when it about to cool out and to evacuate the daily stress. Kinda ambiance always turns in bit of nooky. The men got involved in the game and turn themselves as rent-boys. It was a taboo before; cuz they did make it occasionally. But nowadays men perform as women are doing.

This phenomenon widens and turns in professional work far from prying eyes. A perverted area as those of women, we always find men ready to make everything to earn money. When you visualize kinda activities; you can think that misery turns kinda people in fragile persons. Their motivations varied as those of women.

Anyway we all know either they are doing it for money; for pleasure or in having financial problems. They are special men that we can't meet everywhere.

They often frequent specific areas; where they are sure to meet people who looking for their services. Up to this level of prostitution between men, the violence is omnipresent and lived as routine. The gigolos swim in the same water; kinda business becomes democratized as trivial things. Kinda work aligns itself in the prostitution's lines; which no longer shocked others. Kinda sexual intercourse is often achieved away from nosy eyes. The actors of kinda mess are young boys in the quest of material stability. Often; kinda quest turns in tragedy till the murder and blackmail.

Cougars are looking for hustlers; by all means for the reason that we all know. When you are hearing 'em justifying themselves; it seems that kinda transaction became trivial; and the affection got price. In the gigolos side it's the same history as common women; the lure of the superfluous; trying to get things they can't afford.

They all practice the forbidden attitudes; even have a pact with the Tempter; a major risk to being trapped by the dirt and fast cash.

Kinda activity has been chosen by kinda people; who have been engulfed in poverty's wind. But kinda bitterness obliged most of them to be without dignity.

Even some people are telling; even with suffering; there are some people who keep their dignity intact. It seems this belongs to the past, because of the scarcity of kinda trend. To lure and amaze kinda women in the quest of fresh meat, every gigolo has his tactic. Some of these gigolos approach kinda women and introduce themselves as guide. When the woman does not refuse; they use another technique, they dredge her. There are other men without falter.

They come straight in the matter, proposing them to get some tail; as if they know what brought these women in seaside resort. Devilish contracts which straight emerged from the devil: you take care about me then I shall offer you everything you want. Kinda women in lack of love and sex have a serious reality behind them.

Most of these women have been trapped by some harmful instigators; throwing them in parity history. In that way; the most enthusiast women don't realize a thing goes for being replaced by another constraint. Some men fight against the parity that some women reclaim; in mistreating them at home; or do not being serious in the couple, in wooing every woman they met. You can imagine kinda dirt and crazy deceptions behind all these negative love affairs. Some men prefer turn aside, when they meet kinda women who live through parity way. In that lane they took; some women live in constant difficulties to find the durable relation; because of their negative character. As one goes along they get laid with these studs, they fell in love and became easy prey.

Without doubt the difficulties and iterative misunderstanding will knock behind the door to turn the situation worst. In that fear to lose the man, some women strive concretizing the relation by the positive. When they are cheated by the men; remembering about their expenses and the sincere love they are manifested.

They all often turn up hysteric. We all know that the world became a huge distraction park; a gigantic park of distraction; for people who are looking for hot sensations. Kinda tourists stream in seaside resorts in the quest of flesh as vampires. They look for available flesh and obedient for all kinda practices. Numerous among them wanna reflect a good image, in telling they only wanna contribute in the development of these poor countries. Human's bodies; tourists have it as they want; without being worried by local authorities who welcome them as saviors. In numerous countries; who pays the piper, calls the tune; cuz he contributes to development. That's him who brings the money; it's why he's considered as the master in the area; during the stay.

Peeps go spare cuz of failures and mores been touched. To succeed, you must fornicate; a reality that some areas can't deny nowadays. Several people are trapped into that system of fornication named prostitution of any other kind. The veiled prostitution is everywhere nowadays until some workstations.

Countless scandals; some professions encounter it, as the modelling; it is a risky profession. You often see the profession turns in clandestine prostitution; when the fashion-show ends. Numerous modelling agencies have been involved in women trafficking; an act that turns in pimping. When kinda initiative comes into sight; most of women find themselves trapped in that dirt that they nothing done to avoid.

Businessmen and some politicians like kinda spectacle, cuz the nooky is guaranteed; and highly performed. It is a form of behavior that the law strictly forbidden. A succulent gift for kinda men and this procedure is normal, if things go to their favor. Anyway the hypocrisy is everywhere; women launch in kinda adventures without mastering the conception of kinda universe.

Most of them are greedy and can't perceive the trap behind the scenery. Most of em silliest; believing pledges and the role of star they can embody in the idiot box. They will know the charm of misery and desolation, the day that they will be entrapped into that manipulation.

The lure of gain ruined most of them. That profession crackled and shown another face; some women have been constraint to make forced prostitution. Constraint in these unholy games, by ruthless people who only seek money as them; and same time augment the influence of the devil. The roads of world are crowded by desperate women; who often created their negative situation, by lack of discernment.

Most of them are forced to get involved in a universe that they can't master. Most of women are unintelligent; if you carefully follow the trajectory they took to lead their life, and getting props. Most of men know it's really easy to fool 90 percent of them because of their frame of mind. Countless women became merchandises in world's eyes; and most of them have anymore the choice and run the risk, do not get out from it without troubles.

Most of these women abandon the quest of the liberty every time, when this infernal spiral comes into sight. You can see everything and everyone in kinda trafficking; even married women.

There are some among them whom their husbands turned in professional prostitutes; as we already said. There are some women whom their husbands don't know the persecution that they are living. Beyond repair hits the family door, often their wives yield, when the fella has deep pockets. No doubt; they lose the wife, who gets pleased of that situation. That's beyond of some people's ken they become bystander.

These women whom their husbands turned in prostitutes have been the victims of vicious mentality. Knowing what these women were looking for; they suddenly appear as curer to relieve their ardent desires. Instead of seeing the light; they are facing a sort of endless dark tunnel. When some among them see the light; you can see them create associations to fight kinda criminality. Whilst some among them try to feedback; others strive to annihilate kinda tragedy from their mind; deciding to melt into crowd.

They took this step to find an honorable way out. Myriad works have been created and lots of towns have been renovated via the human trafficking. So the prostitution became indispensable in this era, for some people to have sex relations and for others to have a job of all kinds. According some people the prostitution harmful it can be; is an efficient cure against the misery. In some countries; instead of selling their culture, kinda people sell the sex for nymphomaniacs to fight against devaluation or financial crisis.

The pornography is on the same wavelength and performed in another manner. Its industry is really powerful; cuz the pornography attracts dangerously; and more by curiosity. The influence of pornography spreads wide-world and inflates every day. They are specialized in obscene scenes with sadism. You can hear or visualize lots of shits, kinda perversion that a normal human being can't accept into the conception of his life. The zoophilism; scatology etc...That's only a little part of this huge platform of mess.

Kinda fetishism manifests none limit and can bring people into the non-conceivable. Bondage until the incest a disgusting universe, where other practices come appending into that extreme squalor. Just hear how kinda dirt are performed; can give you chill in the skin; when you try imagining what God can think about that; and different castigations this may engender. Most of people drowned into this phenomenon consciously. Whatever men or women, most of 'em became chauvinistic of blue movie; blue movies of all kinds. The smut is really appreciated by countless people; whilst religions strictly banned this state of mind.

A real perversity they are performing and are very conscious about their doings. A foul conception of life, they are infusing with flippancy; their conception is a real pong and defies all logics. Initiatives and perceptions instigated by their master Beelzebub "the lord of flies". Kinda people have their minds darkened, soiled and kept in the nihility. Immature to see the rawhide or don't give a damn 'bout the eternal whiplash; they lined up in sadism and nymphomaniac lines.

Even they got alterative purpose, we shall keep through our little minds that they all put their signs in devil's emblem. They all fucked up since they step in Beelzebub's den, the brainwash reached paroxysm then thrown 'em in the deviant conception. All that after the Supreme-Being gave the first positive steps then warned us 'bout z-Old-Nick's manigances. Day to day they turn in devilkin, when they are in their squalid hide. You ain't fizzle out, when you are gremlin. Look them gaped, when they figured out that this member of the family belongs to the banned clan. And yet they were hobnobbing together and every day, judging him by his normal mien, whilst he was behaving as everyone.

Got 'em red-handed; most of 'em affirm with desolation to be the victims of the lord of flies" bullshit". As we predicated, you obligatory meet the dark face of internet everywhere you perceive the banned things. The recruitment of actors and actresses is most of time done in its platform. You can see kinda people performing scenes with dogs; or with excrements.

Indescribable squalid; some adepts are trying to give a sense. They all purported to be innocent and do not like kinda sadism; but gloss over when they see these base practices. They all purported to be innocent and do not having alternative, whilst constant flaks are throw on 'em then became eternal label. You ain't innocent of what you're doing. Some of 'em pictured the devilish contract then figured out what were waiting for 'em. They won't anymore out from easy wampum, the whirlwind from the lure of gain straight in 'em. Straight to the evidence; the virtuous peeps became overwhelmed and desolated by kinda findings. Inured mind required do not pass out, when hidden files in daylight. The non-initiated minds try to cotton on the unintelligible.

They thought themselves [how they can do things of kind] without lick it, cuz never you will twig, when the hell-kite uses them as puppets on the strip. The mutation is here, no deny possible, a real misunderstanding for inefficient clans that dare it.

Colleens ain't the only ones who've been trapped in zoophilism universe; numerous fellas perform in this Old-Nick's game. Worst is kinda persons could be peeps next door; but the mask tears open all of sudden, when opportunity comes into sight.

What saying 'bout the scatology, one of the extreme levels of sadism; where the adepts must paint all their bodies with humans or animals dejections; then eat it. Altered minds embody that grime then embraced the crass ignorance. Pornography has been built on levels linked with fervent adepts attracted by diverse practices. As the fervent followers of urology or the bondage; practice that lures some people who like exerting physical suffering to have cry of pain from the prey.

You can picture them drooling over, when they 'bout to inhale cry of suffering. Kinda spectacle throws adepts through an indescribable universe. The thing turns 'em enthusiastic as demons. According some persons the pornography is classified on 3 areas; the classic, sadistic or fetishist. The classic form was kicked downstairs, cuz are looking unholy sensations.

Same time kinda peeps went toward sadism and fetishism; cuz they found there what they were looking for, after tasted all kinda sensations. The sadism incites people to throw money down the drain unconsciously. In lack of affection, most of 'em subscribe themselves in devil's page web.

The foxiest among 'em used tactics to get involved in the game, and to have things free via internet. The images of these sexual excesses give pleasure to adepts and turn the non-concerned repulsive. Kinda practices have been forbidden by the law; but the tapes of kinda practices are sold as scones, and are viewed by non-reliable to suspicion people. Non reliable to suspicion people that you must got red-handed to identify them. The pornography limited itself to describe sexual relations between men and women who constantly live in the libertinage. Most of them came in this area by the lure of gains.

Indications of that kinda practice were taboo; but became a drug for sympathizers. Most of men have fear to see their girlfriends or wives flee in the direction of easy money; or to stumble into demon hocus-pocus. Dangerous drug that we disregarded, cuz most of us enjoy full of it and turn hooked. Nobody takes the time to see or to find the cure for the dying world. We can't evaluate the damages that the pornography may engender in some maniac brains.

Kinda vices can metamorphose people in sadist till incite them to achieve rape and atrocious crimes. Most of these shortcomings were in 'em since adolescence. They only spit what inside 'em. The erotica ruins our relation with God. Nowadays everything is based on ruse, whilst the fight versus Satan's army turns in attrition war, cuz enemy always rises from the dead, when they got defeat. A balance research and a fight filled of traps; as we said only a man of God with a constant help can show the way; where are located genuine things; those crated by God and those imagined by the ruse of human.

We really regret that mutation of the human's soul and their disconnection with positive signs. We can worry about it, cuz we know where that thing came from, and its end. Another concern the partner swapping; several persons like it and consider it as sexual practice; then adopted kinda gender orientation consciously. The vices led most of 'em into that negative concept till changed partner awhile is no longer disturbing for them. Several couples heading blind into that dark aspect of curiosity then turned in swingers.

They annihilated the decency to light the forbidden. Incomprehensible for the non-initiated, cuz trying to implement the decent philosophy that hardly sees the light. Break the routine is the cause, several adepts shouted loudly, whilst other adepts concealed it deeply. Dark mental-makeup, they really like the deceitfulness. Some people step into kinda nonsense, they wanna experiment salacious experiences. They assumed that odd sexuality.

Trapped into the influence of duplicity, some peeps found a way do not longer get a hide, when they go wild and to be honest with the partner. A dangerous trap, for those who were not involved in such practices; most of them have been trapped by forbidden pleasures. They found themselves trapped in such vicious cycle, either by vicious mind; by odd curiosity or the constant angst to see the partner goes looking for peeps of his clan. Where is the difference between the partner-swapping and extra marital relations? The partner-swapping is often practiced in some strategic areas; in swinger's club or often in the house of an adept.

We ain't mentioning some places that hosted kinda odd meeting as nightclubs, restaurants etc.... Most of time they hid their gender orientation and to escape from criticisms. People turned loco then impose all their dirt fantasies to the society. Countless among them turned straightforward then dare blow wide open what they want; when they want, and the way they wanna that the world moves.

Everyone strives to lure the fellow citizen to be at the same kind. We're joking, peeps misbehave far from prying eyez; but before God's eyes. Nowadays people got guts to render most of their activities transparent, the infidelity turns prima facile. Sins are noticed as booming activity; that's no longer shortcomings but a legitimate desire. We can't settle an exact number about peeps who fall into the duplicity trap, but the trend is hallucinating.

Some men throwing wampum down the drain. Often they cognize, sometimes they don't cognize they indirectly incite tarts to have lucre. A so called benefit, not knowing they are infatuated with uncouth females and exposed to illness. A working girl has more value an' esteem than kinda crooks.

Some females disappear, they forgone you, cuz you facing the schtuck. Brainy blokes observing several chicks become bawds and manipulators. Cuz of dearth they became gifted to entrap easy prey. Eyeing their contrivances, they achieving cunning strategist, jilted you when you're kaput. Forthwith tempted to get another sucker, no doubt this one will be the next prey.

Some men assured that the most asinine among men is this one that wenches mislead, is always the case? Cuz often the most street smart find himself trapped in some damsels' trap prior he gets the picture. They are full of shrewdness to cozen her circle of acquaintances, no mercy when they got money dearth.

Push 'em aside if you sussed out the confidence trick, better for you to get 'em sussed out. Cuz these streetwalkers will ruin your life emotionally and financially. Prior get your oats, you gotta highlight the mazuma. Some feeble men are in conflict with their parents, cuz of some not reliable women. Parents see the trap then wanna prevent it, but often the men are not able to outflank these manipulators. Feeble men prefer face their parents then to lose friends just to be with their girlfriend, if I dare naming kinda women girlfriends. When you are beside kinda woman, her current thoughts are on the one she really loves secretly. Either she can't get the man for diverse reasons or they meet each other in hiding to stir keepsakes, so stay safe.

Same thing can happen to women. Most of women became really proud and freestanding about everything that relates their daily life. Their financial situation is not insignificant. Nowadays they no longer fear to get serious sanctions from the husband or boyfriend when they cheated.

They became obsessed by the beauty and fashion; most of 'em seem do not understand that appearance is ephemeral. They spend all their time strive to appeal to men, even being married. The infidelity was a taboo, cuz everyone had feared to be got red-handed, cuz the shame was guaranteed. But nowadays the duplicity turns in fulfilment. Several women affirmed like that situation too much; they like the philandering men; grim conception. Several men stepped into that game, whilst other men have fear sanctions from the spouse.

Some men have their life shattered cuz of duplicity. Face to face with troubles, some fellas manifest a discouraged envy meeting genuine wife someday, cuz eye-witnessed that first seekers been trapped negatively, then been paranoid from redoubtable manigances. The remaining I don't mention em, cuz got traumatized minds.

Fear widely in 'em, wenches ablest to shatter the life of fellas in the long run, and then twist around their little fingers as ring around finger. Kinda guys often experienced tumultuous relations, with negative girlies who use whims and blackmail as redoubtable weapon to shatter everything in resistance. A real fella does not fear to miss something he handled before. Someday the bitter lesson straight at their side.

Girlies are in a bit of lack of direction; days go till disgust and troubles appear at their side. Through troubles, emerged some cruel hearts-killers came from nowhere then make colleens live a real nightmare for revenge. Kinda guys turned in gifted players, decide to handle bout 'that veiled naivety from lasses, then throw 'em in a deep and unbearable unbalance to eye 'em suffer. Your misunderstanding and suffering here; fallen in love after achieved countless years of cheating. Who could predict your negative schemes will have the boomerang effect. The men cotton on most of women no longer reliable, and they turned in skilled gold digger. Some men told they misbehave to get avenge from their early misadventures. All these histories stink nothing sincere and serene.

Some persons assured things turned of kind cuz of duplicity, and then pointed straight troubles that wind couples. Can't expose it as current cause, some of us define kinda statement as welter of words; cuz peeps used to handle bogus then turned it in misleading talks to shape alibi. The analysis of kinda prob is really down to earth; women turned in another version of men. Nowadays most of 'em in the cheating spiral, then out from there gifted and so perverse.

Men been outstripped by women's skill. Into thicken fog these nymphomaniacs minds are deeply trapped, till told they truly handle positively the love, of course the devil's love. Love has no meaning in peeps' eyez, when they first strode line of devil's den, but turned in another definition, when the word has been taken from god's area. Kinda step notifies the lightness of human's strategy in all aspects. The pornography; the vices that some serials infused in fragile minds are the outcome of iterative wind of bitterness and despair.

Anytime the idiot-box broadcasts serials on which themes are 'bout shattered couples that spending time on destructive cheating. Indecency broadcasted before viewers as efficient hypnotizer, they often unable putting things in perspective.

79

Most of them hurry to go performing the negative from motion pictures. Forget virtuous mores; cuz that's no longer attract, whilst duplicity gained ground and advances with a curious pace that peeps really initiated. Yes; most of chicks are cheating as most of men, evil ruined em. In that vicious game; kinda fellas lost their cheating skills.

We are astounded then wondering how most of women turned manipulators and losing words that qualified 'em pure and worthy. In the most couples; bizzle decides about everything. In the street some men turn as lion; but once at home these same men turn in wimp. Kinda men see their life tuned in hell; their girlfriends or wives twist their little finger roughly every day. The shame is on these men; who refuse to neglect kinda women who only bring negative. When a chica tries to sweat you, cuz she thinks being a knockout; leave her abruptly. Her frame of mind is immature as her beauty is ephemeral. She can turn landmine in the long run then become pray for genuine men.

The notion to be in couple most of men and women don't know. The couple is a reciprocal deal linked with the respect. A conception soiled by a daily manipulation, and which is crackled everywhere. You can see men who concentrate all their energy; on a wench who is not reliable. They prefer lose everything to bring this woman on bed, cuz they perceive her as a knockout. You all are really blind; the woman loses her beauty, when you discover her the first night. When the curiosity is killed; all the rest turns in fantasy. The infidelity is practicing by several manners.

3 ways been noticed the sexual touching; online chat; the sexual act. The major part of that dirt history is performing on the net, under several forms; there are some we can't list and explain. Most of between them; either men or women are cheating on the net; chatting with another partner than their boy or girlfriend. During kinda chat all kinda erotic discussions are performed discreetly. The cybersex is a pastime for hot sensations seekers, discussions about sexual fantasies. Kinda erotica dialogues are very dangerous; cuz that practice incites the duplicity for those who are married and the debauchery.

Often kinda discussions are stimulated by sexual desires as masturbation. Kinda unholy sport attracts several people; a sport on which several people are full time subscribed; married or not. The cybersex turns in hard drug, a harmful phenomenon that several peeps found themselves trapped. Become addict in internet is dangerous; cuz this decreases the performance of someone who doesn't master it. That addiction often contributes in some families' troubles; till turn in divorce. Most of people have no interesting activity on the net. If they aren't in pornographic sites, they often turn themselves in cybersex sites to relieve tirelessly their obsession about sexual desires.

Virtual sexual intercourses; most of people in the planet are deeply victims; the debauchery reached high level, even those who heal them are also sank into detriment of that phenomenon. Internet is a platform of debauchery and total perdition; when you try to explain people its dangerousness; they prefer use the platform as they want.

They doing of kind, cuz musing you are a senior citizen through the spirit; they don't care till get into the dirt troubles. Internet is omnipresent in our lives, more in indescribable lives, when it got them; it turns peeps' sexuality. The internet is a frequent form of the infidelity, cuz it already shattered several couples, ruptured couples as we rive tissue. Even we known that infidelity always before our eyes; but we are really conscious its influence accelerated things. That acceleration allowed them to leave the virtual secret toward unholy reality. Infidelity on the net turns in continuum; secrets relations that throw several couples in total unbalance. Sexual chats with unknowns till specialized forums of discussions, stimulated by lewdness and erotic reflexes that their minds inhale.

The cybersex is a business, in same time it is a worldwide nuisance; a platform where profiting transactions are in motion 24 round the clock. Kinda transactions make some people flee, made them fled cuz knowing the damages behind, if they false step. Others don't care about its dangerousness then don't hesitate to spend, emptying credit card or check-card. They are fooling to relieve devilish fantasies; they don't know yet that the devil turns his adepts entirely poor, and in all aspects. Salacious discussions and in live, striptease etc... every predator got widely what he ever looking for. Overturns from these virtual areas are booming, and sites that feed kinda fantasies get everyday elaborations to turn things very luring.

They are elaborating to aliment the fantasies of people which are increasing; elaborations which are not in God's path, cuz they only act for peeps get pleased. Devilish sites that throw weak minds in the negative then are trying to raise a deep unbalance to get positive mores annihilate. Your eyes can eye extra marital meeting in some sites that overturned the meeting image in a dirt way.

They are striving to get it accepted. The Tempter is really powerful, his powerfulness emanates from people idiocy. It's become very easy to turn people oaf; cuz believing in nothing then are living in total idiocracy. They revolutionized it in high rate of adulterine meeting; they all proud displaying the mess. Even a few among em ain't acting through that way; but their non-acting in that way ain't preventing them do not selling adultery. Peeps are buying without know some of sellers ain't acting as em; but knowing they are taking devil's stuffs.

They only sell to them, cuz knowing they are dealing with idiots. The duplicity practiced through the taboo got annihilated, and then took place the one that is freely practiced and lived with elegance and artlessness. Certain sites gave ingeniousness and boldness to operate some transactions without care about consequences; top secret they are classified. A perverse mafia; all things are done in anonymity, often the age and the sexual gender are required etc.... in that level the lies are often topical just to being allowed into the sites, for some minors.

Another world in a world; where all kinda perversions are feeding; then adepts get pleased. They don't have only peeps who have frivolous mental-makeup; but among them all kinda mentalities. Of course adulterine sites ain't gratis for kinda nymphomaniacs who prefer relieve stress in demon's side.

They prefer to spend money on it, but turn penny-father when it about to assist the relatives, or bums in the streets who face a bitter everyday struggle. The education failed; youngsters' receptivity became boredom reality. Youth turned in prey in a world of all kinda hazards. Most of people don't know the sense of virtuous word; they haven't initiation about it. The loss of cultural references emanates of that dereliction then manifests itself by a terrible comportment disorder. The fidelity is a positive virtuous which no longer have value in that new schema initiated by the globalization.

A virtuous more that always stands against vices and the practices of infidelity. The fidelity is a loyalty; a positive mentality to preserve a positive comportment in a purpose to annihilate the evil.

The vice is a harmful habit then had as purpose to delete the positive spirit. The virtuous mores should be inside us and must be always regenerated for do not stumble into the negative cycle. The infidels are in a bit of lack direction and have none constancy in their spirits.

The fidelity is a serious engagement in all pacts that involves an oath, and a constant positive attitude. A kept promise is an authentic way to manifest the fidelity, whatever hindrances and the last of that one. Most of em are cheating right and left; whilst all their shortcomings speaking, no doubt that attitude they performing in silence propelled them in the fornicators. In that world of perverse ideas, the wedlock and the fidelity have no longer unanimity.

90% of engagements ain't respected by people; in these days men and women are able to forget the relation that links them with their spouse to go fornicate right and left. To avoid engagement it's to flee from responsibilities. The unhappy love affairs are current in people's life, and most of them turn diabolical the day they decide to act as traitors.

Most of people have no time to care about fidelity; to feel free as bird in a sky; do not render account then to authorize the infidelity inside their minds is adopted. They all rubbed the wrong way, since they considered the fidelity annoying. They classified it in archaic values, and are fighting for that the fidelity doesn't take place in that devilish era.

Most of us are fickle in their daily behavior, a dangerous mien. People can't understand kinda comportments. Where begin infidel comportment; where it gets ends? Most of people can't define it; most of them think the infidelity is only to have sexual intercourse with another partner who is not the spouse. Some salacious talks with another person virtually or not are a dirt form of infidelity. Some people think that the infidelity can turn in virtue nowadays, I can't tell it, but we aren't so far from kinda unholy initiative. All ways bring toward that dirt, we already know it.

Most of trustworthy people who really believed on fidelity and led struggle for that, settled avenge plans, cuz they are victims of shit-stirrers. Some people think peeps gotta flirt right and left then to fornicate to become stable in that life. They all calling for multiplying relations with girls or men; they will tell "he is a git" when you play the honest guy. By fear, they will persuade you to be careful about the manner you will launch on future prospects.

Shammers ruined objective mentality, till they feed negativity. They became versatile through their spirits; cuz crossroads incite that terrible ambiance. Most of people are buying papers which only display the showbiz; perhaps to keep the most idiots dreaming, an area that every day affirms its mindset and its worse vices. Environment, where the adepts change partner like they want without shame neither have rear thinking. The virtuous is synonym of veiled offense in that area. They all the time linked with judiciary universe.

The only masters are sex and money and turned those who hold it influential. The chosen time for lackeys to behave as clowns behind kinda people. They just wanna have their share of the pie then outside they try to matter. To have sex with the girl of another one is an exciting game and became trivial. A stooge will remains a stooge, even he tries playing a valorous game outside. Kinda persons could be married several times like nothing happened before. Sex is everywhere and venerated dangerously. The shekel is venerated as something supreme.

Kinda life they wanna live; they are assuring that kinda life ain't attracting them, but spend considerable time to scrutinize on it. Several women are lured into an odd system, it's why most of em ain't able to discern and their couples get constant troubles. They became greedy, whilst the men become outstripped by events. Kinda circumstances are lived hardly by honest minds, and that conception of life is always topical. You even can lose your wife or girlfriend, if she does not have discernment, worst is when she does not love.

Several women wear expansive and luxury things; they don't work and haven't activity or current activity. The parents of kinda girls who are attracting by the bling can't afford their daughters' want. All that indecency before the eyes of parents; parents are in deficiency and fled their responsibilities. They often fear to ask for or to reprimand their daughters according their mysterious loots. They have feared that these ones look them down in dissing em (talking about their incapacity to supply them). That new community of young women is into an indefinite need according that new conjuncture.

Conjuncture that turned most of em materialist then propelled them in the world of debauchery. Often when they charm men to have finances, the men ask for a great time. They can't refuse cuz they tremble before wampum; so they have a nooky. Debauchery that some people are asking to reprimand severely, where are these worthy women? Reassure peeps who are looking for sincere love-affairs; they are looking for it, cuz sent in evidence positive step.

It seems at every knocked door there are quarrels and deception. Kinda women who are embodying the era 666 don't hesitate to dissimulate their cheating skills to have credit, when they about to cozen. Most of them think the secret of success is to have string of lovers. They only found that way to project the future. Only a bawdy wench can project the future of kind. You will meet the devil in the long run. The moneyed and wise men, who are looking for stability, hedge themselves against these predators. They hide themselves from 'em and turned in modest men, till the day they come across the trustworthy woman.

Kinda step is the good initiative and strictly remain aloof from these fawns. In having string of lovers, kinda women get into their own destruction at all levels. Only the Supreme-Being knows what found inside hearts, so we ain't soothsayers to prevent kinda troubles. To find the suitable person became jigsaw, cuz ambiguities stick into several relations. It became very easy to win lottery than to have a reliable spouse, either man or woman..

The unhappy thing is peeps have the impression to have currently harmful things through their ways. They blow a fuse, cuz they always lost energy, when it about to avoid kinda quandaries. A negative certitude from the spouse and things turn spooky; most of us like to live in an absolute mediocrity. They prefer the indecency and its harmful aspects than decency. In every path you will meet a reality, reality that can deeply destroy you, if you are not trained for kinda dimension.

There are several women who are incapable to disallow, when men come close to them to woo. They can accept several men, and what will happen in the long run don't interest em. If the man has a good looking, the woman accepts without rear thinking, cuz often she thinks about finances.

There are women who are looking for men to avenge, cuz they have been duped. They see red and decide to entrap men in some destructive situations. Several men stepped into that harmful game, then provided as motive they were duped.

These men and women, who behave of kind don't understand the life and can't picture the consequences of such deed. They are interested to flaunt right and left and to have more life destroyed, but the consequences of their act will be harmful for everybody. Several people are ready to misbehave for a small amount money. What they gonna do, when they will be before a huge sum?

That God protects us from these destroyers; in behaving of kind, they tarnish their image and destroy the life of innocent persons who have the mischance to meet their harmful figures. We can't have a consideration for kinda persons, cuz there is probability they put us in serious troubles. The materialism of women is terrible; nothing is free from charge, to keep his girlfriend became difficult for men who mistook while they wooed a woman. Most of them are pretty, but without moral value. Most of them really like being pampered by men, those who used to pamper them; often arrive to get 'em as spouse. Most of women like gifts, good things which are expensive to show their girlfriends they aren't in the same league.

When a man finances 'em all time and pay attention about their whims, they tremble of happiness then commence the manipulation. In that instant, they think they are really attractive and pretty for anybody. The materialism is not innate; it is deep shortcomings, and a way of life that several people adopted.

The materialism is a personal choice, cuz nobody is born materialist. Most of people are materialist then often collect deceptions, when they meet the cheater spirits. They lured people then mislead 'em for their benefit. They privilege the material aspect instead of your antecedents (your projects, kind of job you doing, just to try imagining discreetly the salary of kinda job. They behave of kind to know, if you can support financially their caprices. Disinterested women ain't numerous; cuz interests took advantage on other women.

Most of women's desires are infinite and for an only dissatisfaction, they can destroy years of cohabitation. How many are they to have neglected their men for strictly material reasons? Often the woman can show ungratefulness.

You can do everything for her, and then tomorrow she goes with another fella as you was useless. Most of women got 2 pockets, an authentic pocket and a holed pocket. The holed pocket will receive the good actions you early achieved; the intact pocket will receive negative actions.

They only need little misunderstanding or they want neglect you; she will brings into light your no positive actions. Most of women forget in the same day positive actions that men done for them, every coming day is a new era for most of them. Several people are shouting everywhere about the poverty, but this ain't prevent them to show off when the occasion comes into sight. Most of them show off, when they able affording something awhile.

You can eye 'em trying to be in luxurious cars, luxurious lounges, and luxurious attires, luxurious supermarkets, in luxurious restaurants, have luxurious hair styles, luxurious watches as if it was the primordial things. People know anymore the modesty or they never know it, but obliged to bear till the day they able to express their real nature.

In the troubles with ambient poverty, people like the opulence as if it's really vital for their survival. How many they are to being lured by the superfluous? The superfluous became a cult for kinda persons, in walking in streets wearing valued stuffs, often they can't afford it. How many they are to have brand new apparatus of the latest generation, then have nothing to eat at home? The priorities been deleted for the advantage of futilities and bling. In that way you will automatically meet looniest women who brought into deep fragile men. They brought 'em into deep, cuz these men have feared to lose their comfort, you make my people laugh at. It is not scarce to see some governments playing exhibitionists

They spend most of their time showing off, displaying through the world their skills, and their latest apparatus. Apparatus which are really expensive and destructive, whilst the population is starved or in the depths of despair. How many they are to drive a latest car, whilst at home the precariousness is a daily routine. They have hang-ups vis-à-vis the look of people.

That situation incites us to think that people are really attracted by the opinion of superiority that people can notify for them. What is the price of that loony mental-makeup? You only need to be in frequented spots or in some events to eye that phenomenon reaches heights. They all like the lushness and often ready to turn transgressor awhile, to have something that turns 'em happy. You will always hear; if I could get it this will be great, but if I can't afford, I will content myself what God gave to me. Kinda statements seem being universal, but really different of what most people are practicing nowadays. Most of time, you find these same persons in perverse offense, just to have a valued things.

In the way that people are wasting, incites some inexperienced people to think they have everything they want and they will be not trapped by the daily anguish of invoices and expenses. Don't be overwhelmed, when you step into their houses, cuz the reality will be incomprehensible; most of 'em are really asphyxiated of debts.

To be debt ridden doesn't break their show-off, but often the situation blows wide open drastically then turns bystanders perplex. The spectators of that disillusionment know that their turn is soon, if they follow same step.

In some case mature people don't turn in prey of futilities, but they all time remain aloof from these modern shits that can turn their life chancy. A responsible person will think about his future and his daily duty instead of sink into vanities. Even when disinterested of those fantasies, we shall have problems, has the more reason to play the interesting and to show off everywhere. In that state of mind emerged again the superfluous; a superfluous with shameless adepts, the conjuncture of course; but the dignity in first.

People like the trend of superfluous; the superfluous is often linked with a veiled prostitution, if the adept is an authentic have-not. Have a string of lovers became a trend for men and women, as if it was natural. They all hide themselves into a fake reality, in promoting the casual lovers.

Even wise minds assured that practice is unworthy; this does not avert the practice remains interesting and lucrative for its adepts, especially for lasses. To have a string of lovers is a dangerous manner of perversity and a dangerous manner of prostitution.

That practice is destructive which has an only goal the one to ruin and to gain profit from the other. Kinda persons are not conscious they are vectors; they don't care about their health, before talk about it, we must assure that they really know the meaning of this word. We can't dare to tell kinda lasses have future in that way, if they continue to cheat in the long run, only the lure of gain veiled their diabolical universe. The goal of the game is to cheat the maximum of men to sate materialist needs. That practice became a principal activity around the world and often can turn in drama.

When they are in bunch of women, most of them think valorizing the capacity they have to make ravage on men. Without shame you can perceive them hang beside different men as hours go by.

That practice became justifiable, when you see how kinda women behave and step deliberately in that daylight robbery. Passionate guys turned easy prey in that destructive practice, orchestrated by devil's daughters. Scarce is the sincere love, but men blow a fuse when they realized they are swallowing up into a terrible tsunami of lies, as we early said. Some men prefer the suicide, cuz incapable to stomach kinda betrayal.

That dirt allows them to earn in a day what a salary can't give them. Those who practice it are negative then don't care about their wealth and their future. Kinda women are really attracted by the lure of gain and they sin everywhere they go. That activity became a principal means to earn money for some between them. That practice became legitimate for kinda women. Kinda wenches make them believe they will lead a sincere relation.

Kinda girls will have the inferno in the palm of their hands the less expected moment. The cheating is a work for these ones. You got constant quandaries, cuz you are a part of the evil facet.

Even they know that one doesn't love them, passionate men insist just to get the female, what kinda love affair you can build in that negative certainty. What saying about men? Some of them are in that vicious game to practice freely their perversity, then to become prey, punished according that unworthy comportment. Kinda people think that the life is a game with levels that they really need to explore by all means, but the sanction behind is bitter.

We notice kinda cheatings and broken hearts are in constant progress, for an only purpose the one to outliving. And yet when you question peeps about these allied of devil, they all turn in angel. Anybody refuse strictly to stick his name beside that practice, even the percentage gave 80% adepts. Some men are accomplices of kinda system, because they finance right and left to convince the woman to become lovers, or to have copulation as we said. Most of women step in to the game and squeeze kinda men as the lemon then leave them in the lurch as vulgar suckers.

Kinda wenches do not hesitate to sell every part of their bodies to reach their goal. Also some men step into the game to make same things as kinda prostitutes are doing. Some of them succeed to destroy kinda women emotionally, and others fail, cuz became trapped in their own game. The trustworthy and the persons of honor can't step into that hazardous jungle, cuz they can sign their decline. The one who thinks that the life is only game, the life will hardly game with him.

Numerous are persons who are living in occasional prostitution. Numerous are parents who don't canalize their kids in the positive way, by lack of authority. Numerous are parents who see their children bring at homes suspect manners and suspect stuff then turn a blind eye on the matter. Kinda commotion that parents don't dare face turned them in mutants. You can see the instigators of consumer society sending advertising, a method to turn peeps blind and idiot.

They turn their desire in major needs; they elaborate an infernal spiral to canalize the readable emotions of peeps in materialist cycle. The human life does not depend on his stance, his means, even he is loaded. The truth is elsewhere, a place that only a pure human being can find with his aura. Hypocrite he is, the human does not admit he acts to impress peeps. You can look them rush up in department stores, when an apparatus is about to being release. Some peeps spend the night beside shopping malls, to be the first to have the privilege.

Some people try all the time to hold things that most of people can't afford. Kinda behavior is widely determined by the will to vie with acquaintances, and then to gain respect everywhere. They ease themselves in kinda mentality to impress, to attract, to lure then to show people who they really are in the society. Even they behave of kind, most of them are in troubles every month, cuz they daily face ceaseless an overdraft. They make out peeps got affected, they launched the second offensive.

All the time they associate their advertisings with well-known persons to lure the most materialist minds. The advertisers made them believe they can realize all their fantasies. The non-stupid persons make out that none acquisition can change what we really are, neither rubs our shortcomings. Knowing that the human being have an eternal dissatisfaction, it seems they wanna bring them into deep. Barely a desire fulfilled another one comes into sight. The human runs behind it, as jackal in the desert. Kids become materialists, most of 'em born into a materialist system. Raised by materialist relatives, their mindset is already shaped negatively.

Kids became targets of advertisers, a way to reach parents, who are penny pincher. The trend got a worrying trajectory; some kids don't falter to use in hiding the credit card of their parents to purchase some stuff, or to steal money. Often in the platform of nternet you can perceive kinda cheating gaining ground. It is not scarce to get into a department store, then to see a child crying all over the place to make his parents yield.

Before the eyes of people, some parents yield, because in their state of mind the refusal to cede is a sort of indication that they can't afford, and then decide to accept the whims. They drive their children into the closed circle of materialism that brings tomorrow unforeseeable mutation. The begging is a dreadful practice and with no way out. The actors of this unspeakable phenomenon become innumerable, and the sex does not matter. You can meet native citizens or immigrants trying to survive in the world streets. Powerless they are the god-fearing man, when he is about to look kinda afflicting spectacle through his eyes. A community banished by most of citizens as if they were a kind of malformation of that new society, a society with negative signs.

They only are looking at 'em to give themselves a sort of fake supremacy. Most of them are not foxy for this negativity serves them as lesson, just to prevent coming troubles for their future life. A miscalculation at the other side, those who try to exploit by all means till embrace the outlaw's mind.

They use extreme recourses to convince kinda have-nots to align at their recreant scheme. They are denuded of faith, the law they know it, but through another definition. Sometimes the trade turns in human exploitation. This phenomenon does not arrange anybody and disturbs some people in certain cases. An extreme request is noted by the passersby, who are submerged of problems in their daily life. Kinda people are at the edge of to blow their top. Most of them walk in the streets to relieve themselves from daily troubles, daily troubles that seem to be an inevitable negative matter.

The evil minds are blithesome, cuz are enjoying when the mess and troubles appear then hit everywhere. Among this crowd of passersby is noticed a total divergence, those who want to give, those who don't enjoy giving and those who have zilch to give. All this divergence under a pretext some of 'em assured that to help em encourage the plague. Undeniable, several profits without being in direct conflict with poverty been noticed in current affairs.

That's right, because so many people step knowingly into begging system without being in direct conflict with poverty. They took Machiavellianism as ally, then sent missionaries in quest of easy money has unlimited duration and full-time. Among these missionaries, you can find young people in age to go at school, the parents of kinda kids are facing misery, till lose positive reflexes. They have no remorse when they throw their children in devil's hands, without taking the time to understand, nor to project their future. In troubles no-one believes the positive things.

This plague is incomprehensible for people who are trying to understand its sense. Of course, it's comprehensible for some people who reside in these countries. Most of em got their eyes embrace a daily poverty of the country and its inhabitants. Of another side there is a total disorder, citizens are abandoned to face their terrible fate, and are looked at as if they were not citizens of the country. Kind of citizens are really treated like waste, but nevertheless useful waste for the non-beggar citizens, and some politicians.

They all try to find a way by this way. Some evil minds pointed the immigration as determinant fact of that mess, cuz in the fair battle; they can't stand in the same league with positive thinkers. They represent a threat of the peace, and then will shelter themselves when troubles break out. During the time the followers of the evil thoughts are enduring the thunder of hate that they have occasioned in every aspect. I believe anymore the crisis, but I believe the scheme of some persons. The world has resources to annihilate kinda fake problems. The twice group love kinda beggars in the intention to give them alms.

Give them alms as sacrifices, cuz the charlatans prescribed them this as cure to get their things positive, according to the countries and the beliefs. Terrifying ambiances who will make you gape, if you are not accustomed of this kinda show. The highest bidder could not hold out. Because every step he achieves, he will find a beggar driving to beg. Sometimes it happens that some people to give till have anymore money.

As all trades the begging has specific levels, and gathered all kinda persons. We can find the young missionaries, disabled people and blind persons. As we know some people have been weakened by the economic situation. But some people are profiting about the negative situation. Everything became hard to achieve in the positive way.

But don't be astounded to see some people sink into the illegal way to earn living. Inefficient authorities, a total incompetence to eradicate all this, cuz it's difficult nowadays to enterprise something. Blind or disabled persons accompanied with kids in age to go at school. Kids they use as daily guide to make money. How these countries think apply the changing in these conditions of extreme slavery. None changing when the system kills citizens.

The benefits of the daily begging transformed most people in talented beggar, as if it was a professional trade. The begging became a trade with well-organized levels. In some countries you can't beg anywhere, unless discharging a monthly sum to the owners of certain zones.

Banal people who are proclaimed themselves owners, in a purpose to have a benefit in this profiting trade. They misbehave before the eyes of the victims who have a choice, the one to discharge this sum, in order to have a license to make their business in these strategic places. This regulation is made to have a license to beg in these zones.

Often you can see the professional beggars in action, because their daily activity is visible, they do not dissimulate what they are doing. What to say about the occasional begging. Elegant beggars who behave as everybody, well dressed, and who melt onto the crowd. Another strategy to beg discreetly, the strategy to approach their victims without creates suspicions around. They use simple and short sentences that predict that they are victim of the begging. This technique of the occasional begging is very practiced and sophisticated. When you see these actors in action, you can be easily trapped, if you are not vigilant.

These techniques consist to expose his problems in an accidental manner "my brother can you help me, I lost my wallet or someone stolen my wallet and have no money to return at home. ......Discreet, soft voices achieved in a very convincing way, all the necessary skills to cheat, professional techniques that few persons can agnize in the first meeting. To catch these people read-handed is difficult. You will understand their technique, when you see them in practice with new victims.

In each technique there is a flaw, the problem of these people is they see countless people per day till their memories become short. Because they forget you instantaneously after delicately emptied your pockets, and their trap turns easy to achieve. People are very afraid of poverty and consider it as jinx. A kinda jinx under a form of Damocles's sword. Poverty is not a terrible jinx, but a painful ordeal for the innumerable people who meet it through their route. It is not insurmountable but requests much for rigor, an absolute courage and an immense faith to be able to surmount it.

Poverty is a wealth, with complicated consequences created by god that the human being cannot cotton on its direction. Only god has the key of the truth relating kinda history, why they eat at their fill and why not others? Only god has the answer. Poverty is a handicap for materialist minds. The poverty turns in an authentic destiny for the humans being who are not lured by the superfluous and by these kinda futilities of that modern life. That modern life seems being unavoidable for anybody for the oafs.

People who are fighting against the materialist system of this modern world are eliminated diplomatically by a category of the society. My opinion concerning all that is, I wanna to say in modern life everything is a simple question of sensation from the disease to the absolute poverty that a human being can run across. All this can't mean that poverty is something positive for a human being, but can be positive if people use it to make their actions through the world positive.

Let's take as example the hunger, when a human being faces an extreme hunger; often he is ready for everything to relieve his pain. But oddest is after relieving his unease with some scran; the suffering becomes non-existent, as if it never happened. The person will not have any constraint consign it to oblivion. The most important of that anecdote is to apply it in all negative events, for an only goal to project the reachable matter. The money incites the megalomania for the non-humble. They don't understand the direction of the life, and its terrible and current rules. Terrible rules that sent several persons in a constant troubles.

Also they don't cotton on how vices can be negative and disastrous, if we don't aware about. But time will speaks, cuz at certain dimension everything will be very explicit for every mind. Sometimes you can meet poor or modest human being living in total harmony. Some among em are living in total harmony because they are conscious about the importance of the life and the human value. All that whilst those who pretend being rich living in irrational problems.

As we already said among beggars there are authentic impostors, some people who are attracted in this trade by the lure of gain. Current breach of trust, people who proclaimed themselves disabled to have effortlessly money. You can see them using persuasive methods to get alms, only an astute person and with charisma and seductresses can achieve kinda performance. One day I give alms to a handicapped person who sat in a corner. Not far from there a brawl breaks out between police officers and rioters. We weren't far from a football stadium, a strategic place to make money.

Minutes later, gaped I was, eyed the disabled cadger blundered about, cuz of tears-gas' sound led by scuffles. Eyed him daunted, looking for narrow escape, fled away bare feet with stirrers. The come to blows put the wind up em. Another case I experienced, a fella I ran across in genus ruta. He came close, and then spit up ordeals he faces. Told, he would reach the capital, and then he's coping to get it possible. Details were elaborated, whilst supplicating the exact sum of the journey.

Retorted him, I could achieve more than its request. Agreed he was with happy mood. We weren't in the same wavelength. I proposed him to follow my steps. Arrived at the ticket machine; I bought the ticket without rear thinking, even if I guessed that it was not his only motivation. I was just looking his eyes, when I handed him the ticket. The guy tried to be poker face. But his eyes altered as opened book, even an oaf could read a deep disappointment of losing a large sum. A sum he could hardly get in a day I suppose. Most of human being became stingy; it's why every sum of money became overriding.

In awaiting the arrival of the train, we start a friendly colloquy. When the train arrived the man was lingering behind, just to get into the train after me. After have a sit, the man gone past me, saying thank you, then get through into the next wagon. After the train parked at the next station, I see the same man on the platform, back to our starting point. He was about to wait for the next train, a train for the return.

Standing at the wrong side, he was at the return platforms; the ticket I bought was a failed trick. The begging in some way can be synonym of violence or badgering. Often you can witness fight breaks out between honest or dishonest beggars.

Dangerous fights, when it is orchestrated by bent beggars. If you're trying to intercede, you will be mugged by these shit stirrers. You will picture the contrivance, when you will realize that's an organized stick up. The kindness can play a trick to people who live in that credence. What to say about the daily badgering, a proceeding that sees the light. You can see men, bag ladies and children of all ages wandering every day in buses, trains or streetcars, using an extraordinary magnetism.

They distributing small papers that they try to hand to all passengers in every wagon. Papers on which are mentioned stories of all kinds. Some people go so far till to proclaim they are orphans, refugees or to say they have three children and their wives are pregnant and they are homeless. Other persons hand small papers mentioning incredible things.

Some persons told they subscribe themselves at the employment agency or they handed curriculum vitae to some companies and are waiting favorable responses. The difficulty is, it's as all circuits, and it became very complicated and saturated. It is extremely difficult to change the manner to proceed, because it's become a problem of area. It's always the same story that coming back and people already used to see them working. In this confusion, people cannot distinguish the true needy and the hypocrite. In some countries they are people who are going to hire poor children from some poor areas, orphans just to accompany them to practice the begging. They behave of kind just for the people to be sensitive with their sad stories. The people who cogitate are wondering, why things became tough?

Cuz the abuse and the trafficking of children became banal. Some people are indifferent when it about kinda trafficking. Some of 'em obliged kids to beg everywhere and all the time, whilst others don't care about, cuz they sink into daily problems.

They all are waving the banner of every man for himself. You must travel everywhere to see the hugeness of the evil. You can see the misery movement, as hive activity. Human's right is no more respected, who care about? Even the persecuted people accept everything to survive, whilst others don't know the content of the human rights and are misled every time.

The strugglers against that discrimination and that mistreatment have assured there will no peace if things move of kind; a citation that everyone between us knows in silence. They prefer do not destabilize the interests of the people who boss em around. There will have no peace if misery and discrimination spread, kinda kids are same than kids of rich people. We denied the difference.

Recently elected some mayors or presidential candidates in the electoral euphoria, declare being the right men for the job, the dirty job. They are trying to lure idiots, till trying to embody the behavior of the tyrant. They promise has who wants to hear balderdash, they will make no exception.

They will eradicate without remorse this plague that tarnished the image of their country. What kinda image tarnished their country? Their current hypocrisy often tarnished their country too. They promised all the citizens will find again the peace and the security they lost without delay. As usual promises were not achieved, or they became weak before the plight. Recently elected some candidates launch a massive repression, in which the human compassion is not topical. After all, what obstacle can stop em, after have been elected for that mc job.

The so called defenders of the law, holder of the ephemeral authority, the authority of repression, don't falter any more, and under a fake pretext to destroy all harmful activities that threat the tranquility of the plaintiff citizens. They indicate the undesirable persons as a wound and sanction them severely, everytime they are into sight. They act as stooge. In some countries, some elected persons emitted decrees to prohibit the beggars, and all people they judge useless for the towns.

The people targeted by these decrees are considered as harmful and who threaten the public peace! Worse it will be, if they do not present any hygiene, because they will divert haughty people of their way. They are often drunk, they beg, steal and attack the passers-by; complains shouted by several plaintiffs. Designated as shit stirrers, these future applicants accept all sort of dirty pacts to be elected. They use these false pretexts to have an insignificant power.

Some of them don't believe values they are defending, but shout everywhere to show the contrary. The arguments they think defending are not genuine). In this context, they launch a kind of manhunt, a manhunt carried in an unexplainable manner. A manhunt that everyone got his own opinions (the right persons and those who are only living to defend their interests and the rest doesn't mean. Some people are very happy about kinda procedure, led with a humiliating manner by people who are very thirsty of power. They are doing all this to have recognition in the worldly.

They wanna step into closed clan of bourgeoisie till embody the evil in all its aspects. Often kinda procedure turns in blunder, because often the police is designated to achieve kinda unworthy task. Some people come to a conclusion about this subject "this fear and this refusal of the difference, is only a hidden racism. Kinda initiative throws a dark veil on the guilty persons of that situation.

Some people and politicians embody that attitude of tyrant; their clan throws a countless number of people without defence in the street. Kinda attitude widened the number of people the most touched by ceaseless misfortunes. Ceaseless misfortune of that modern life, human being is often instigator. There are people who are not agree with the begging, but they do not accept the methods to eradicate it.

In some countries the beggars are directly excluded from the touristic areas, and public places. Strangers or natives of the county haven't importance; they will meet the same fate.

Often this kind of reprimand widens when the public opinion are favorable about that discriminatory initiative. Most of us perfectly know the state of mind of the majority of the politicians and some negative people. To get into action then to show his political commitment everyplace, hypocrite engagement just having the time to obtain what one wants.

They do not hesitate to raise all the small whims coming from the majority of the voters, till the most idiotic whims. The political parties are in permanent electoral campaign, and their favourite theme is the insecurity, and other current events which are suitable for them to throw the citizens in constant fear. They have the bad habit to foment a psychosis of violence or insecurity everywhere in the country just to convince. The right people should be protected, only the idiots can believe it. All these initiatives are in concordance with a police State and this arsenal of repressive laws.

That's their conception of life, whilst their adversaries pointed them as renegade states. Myriad laws came out; these laws have been established by certain presidents of the republic. Kinda presidents of the republic were clever and effective; or who were believed themselves effective. Clever they were, cuz they succeeded to fool people every time they wanted. They currently have what they want from people without meet difficulties. To fool people is the most easy that a human being can achieve, cuz the human being is often lured by the soft lies. Myriad laws enforced, but laws been wrote by humans; reliability is not their deep quality if wampum into sight.

They had promised and they had the obligation to act. But all their so-called laws that came out showed their total inefficiency, because a new adverse clan doesn't care about that. The most vigilant people realized the ceaseless manipulation. They step aside from these manipulators, who progress because of the lack of knowledge of the majority of these citizens.

They understood that they can count only on them, because every man for himself, even the great boasters. During this time, some people who are denuded of good sense and positive perceptions are absorbed into soft lies and incoherent fantasy, handled like a drongo. Other side we found disconnected youth, who often care about their image and about the modernity. The youth has been lured in the cult of unconsciousness and the unconcern. That situation is the trigger of a repetitive failure. As if negative files ain't enough, the smuggling comes add itself.

Another trouble and became a trivial matter, harmful and very disturbing practice, which is in the way to throw the economy of several countries in troubles. The reach of this phenomenon makes unproductive honest investments around the world. Potential investors became very discouraged, very annoyed and very anxious, because of this new illegal way to earn living. Illegal manner to earn living, that practice is defended by lazy persons to have money pronto. Principle of least effort is their deep conviction.

With this practice which is booming, it is very difficult to estimate the negative effects that smuggling entails in the economic field of countries which are deeply affected by this scourge. What is sure from doubt is; it became very difficult to fight against this scourge, because of this financial crisis. As if these people pointed as masterminds of these networks are untouchable, often only journalists in hidden camera can approach and investigate within their networks, often with their consent. There are people, who fight against smuggling, but this is not always the case in several countries of the world, cuz the plight left em no alternative.

The effects of this negative situation tossed some governments in a tight struggle. Outstripped some governments take the step of inaction; often accomplice they boosted gradually the luring of the smuggling and his supporters. Smuggling widened and has conquered several versatile minds, because it attracts people toward a quick conquest of benefit. I would not say that this practice began to be legalized, but I'll just say it starts to take its place in most corrupted companies.

A way to survive in this plight, they hardly deny it. It became inevitable for kinda companies to step into smuggling; they are struggling to survive, in order to make a name in the future. Some trustworthy companies are facing this worrying development which will influence them negatively in the long run. The survival of commercial and industrial activities became very threatened. And several investors have alerted authorities concerning their protection, fear for their decline in this invisible struggle, which is growing and beyond their competence.

They have opponents on the other side, treacherous companies that constantly increase their strength, according the number of followers they attract every day because of the plight. Smuggling is undoubtedly an injustice and a loss for those who have based their businesses in the legality. The practice of the smuggling became highly visible, even if a minority struggles against. This minority just tries intervening; in dissuading adepts of smuggling do not step into smuggling business.

The struggle is very difficult, cuz the smuggling adepts think the smuggling is the only solution to escape from a puzzled system. The fraud does not afraid them, cuz everybody makes illegal things on other matters of life. But by their negative actions, they are unaware that they are projecting the world towards an economic and industrial disaster. Kinda disaster can contribute later to the loss of everyone. As smuggling, counterfeiting is very annoying for manufacturers, and very interesting for traffickers who operate in this field of activity.

Behind this illegal activity are hidden underground organizations, which are established around the world. This traffic turns happy half of the world population, because they find something out of it. About the treacherous companies, their activities and survival are not directly threatened. The attitude shows the way to behave in businesses, "every man for himself, the goal is to escape by all means. Many people feed their families through this illegal traffic.

During this time the economy takes serious blows, and that the worthy manufacturers turn sicko by seeing all their works losing value. Through this modern war that seems to be declared the customs service know this deterrence has no effect and perhaps never will be. This mess took them to achieve a blitz in some spots they deem very doubtful. In these troubles emerged

the world of the homeless persons, a suffering and a constant lack of consideration. You can see there, same discrimination, a non-frequented population by the citizens of this new era. Kinda unknown population attracts nobody or a population that people do not dare to approach. When misery is evoked the thoughts go directly at the world of homeless persons. It is not always the case, when intelligent people use their thoughts in a logical way.

The rise of unemployment, the lay-offs throw more and more people in the street. That's a dubious world; a world one which we can't know the following of events (aggressions, brutalities, more sordid the one than the others are often noticed.

A brutal game linked with punitive expeditions orchestrated by people whom the system has destroyed. Most of them behave of kind just to have of what to eat, or to have a bottle of beer to drown problems the time of one evening. The homeless persons are numerous nowadays, and to know their exact number is complex.

The figures are in constant augmentation, and the people who follow them have the discouraged feeling that each day the number increases. In this population which is excluded from the system, we find there any kinds of people, men, women and children who sleep on the ground. More terrifying in the world of the homeless is each one has his history (the true reasons which have thrown them in the street. To be homeless is often tied with total poverty or loss in value. Among these people who have been excluded from the society, there are those who struggle for always staying in the ship of the current life. Among these people who struggle, the majority between them have a professional situation, but not having flat because of an ambient shortage of housing.

Some among them cannot claim housing, because not having a current address then to be accepted as normal citizens. They live from day to day, without to be able to control the destiny of the following day. Because the only certainty is that tomorrow this will be a similar stinky struggle. We can notice an infernal cope that seems interminable In wintertime some buses are chartered to take homeless people to help centers. They are sent over there for that they avoid the dangers of the winter.

All these actions are made with a purpose to help them, and not to die in the cold then propose to them some scran. But two things are very astonishing, because each time you see a no fixed abode being collected in street; it is not scarce to see him again in this same place the following day. Second thing the most astonishing is that most between them systematically refuse to follow their so called rescuers to the lodging houses chartered for this kind of event.

They refuse to get there, cuz some of them have gotten bitter souvenirs, when they spent night in these spots. The few remaining do not accept according to the reputation and the environment of these spots. Most of people described kinda spots as places with total insecurity. We can project the apprehension to go o' there, because all types of individuals go in these places.

According the sayings of certain people, it would seem that kinda places are without security and the crazier reign supreme. Several among people throw a constant challenge to the innumerable games of chance. The motivation of that excitement is to strive till to have a place in kinda life. Kinda people launch themselves into a world of despair. They have a terrible obstinacy and a ferocious envy, in trying to be on the top of the hazards, a manner to have a feeling of power and a control that they can't have if they do not step into this spiral of games.

The proliferation of games of chance and betting sites on Internet turns the creators of kinda games richer to the detriment of dependent persons. The games of chance became a terrifying dependence, which is in the same rank as those of the drugs or other substances of addiction. More in more people are putting all their hopes, beliefs and energy on the games of chance, instead of helping the players to have a time out, games of chance drive them into deep. All this excitement, because they can't arrive to make ends meet.

So many among them no longer reluctant to use the online games of chance, cuz they are easy access and discreet. To have an access to get into these online games is very easy; you just have to bring the bank card. With this addiction, some minors do not hesitate emptying gradually and quietly the bank cards of their parents, if by mistake they leave them lying around. A law prohibited to minors to play games of chance, but that one ain't efficient and are not applied by people.

As we all know nowadays, the laws are difficult to apply, even if they are enforced, there are always means for people to circumvent it. Internet is one of them, because how many juveniles hide their age, when they enroll on the online betting sites. Therefore, as we've seen, it became very easy to bypass certain laws via the Internet. And yet in some sites, there are barriers to prevent minors to get access through. But its barriers are very light and ineffective, to prevent the participation of minors. The people no longer have to search so long to find games of chance online.

Nowadays these games invade our screens, and come into sight under the form of advertisement. These advertisements are of all kinds, games of chance, pornographic. All those diabolical spasms coming en masse, and it is very difficult to get rid of one of these tabs. It's hard because if you try closing one of these advertising pages, another one opens automatically. As if they force you to get into this curiosity, which may be destructive in the long term.

Most people are betting on all types of events, often most them are freezed before their television or spending all their time in the tobacconist's in the hope of gain. But most of the time their expenditures are not limited on the games, but all this stress is accompanied by incessant cups of coffee, cigarettes, expenses which in a week represent a no negligible budget. The gaming industry became very profitable for the creators of these games of all kinds. Kinda games became universal and by the same occasion attract several adepts through the world.

The new generation has games of chance in the blood, because the economic context leaves them no alternative. Nowadays the world is plunged in the era of the addiction. A world of consumption which shown no limit and the game is tolerated, and even encouraged the excesses and the abuse of all kinds. This attitude is very disturbing which has a tendency to incite the most unconscious toward imaginary challenges, and the research of the supremacy by all means.

The attractions that people shown for an immediate success, have thrown many of them in the grave or in genius ruta. This way of seeing things don't incite them to wonder why the majority of people have exceeded the line of the indebtedness, till to step into excessive debt. The people are no longer need to cope with the addiction, and have the attraction of philistinism in the blood. And by the same occasion became very powerless within worldly, which incited most of them in an extreme dependence. The dependency is a real danger and omnipresent, because it became a virtual pleasure and a way out for people in difficulty or not.

Some people are a little aware of the real danger that lurks, but they do not arrive to disengage themselves, and often involve the doctors to have some help. Most of the people know they are in danger but this does not prevent them to stop, because they reached the point of no return. To stop their virtual world will cause an imbalance with unforeseeable after effects for most of them.

Because their passion leads them till a total loss of control and their good sense, then throws them through constant destructive sanctions. In another aspect of life, we also find certain realities through the world which are overwhelming; in some spots of the world, people are ready to make everything for success. A success which does not emerged from a true knowledge, but more in Machiavellian tricks. Nowadays the success is synonym of incessant and infernal hardships; kinda hardships that the most unfaithful people achieve indecently to make ends.

Because they know the success is no longer linked with the true values of intelligence, but with darker and deeper realities that a mouth can't divulge without make chills through some skins.
Success bothers because the road to success is littered with ill-intentioned persons, ready to do anything to give you the worst obstacles. Sometimes you will face some plots that could affect you the rest of your life.
Some people never let you succeed, when they face difficulties or jaleasy in em. This world is no longer for positive people; the modernity notifies them there is no longer a land for righteous minds.

Because evil spirits gaining ground in this new era and at the same time will destroy everything in the most basic mistakes. The spirits without discernment will suffer. The positive people are sidelined in this new era, because their way of living and to proceed disturbs the spirits of the destruction. This lack of morality and this lack of value are in the height in a world in distress, the instigator of this chaos is Satan. Satan has as acolytes conscious and unconscious people, but when you spy all their deeds they all seem unaware. We don't talk about conscious acolytes, because they have chosen Satan's chamber and his allies, but rather of unconscious peeps.

We talk about them, because they are a actors and actresses of this world, (those who do not have the capacity to think correctly then follow the waves of negative as abandoned flock of sheep in desert.

Flock of sheep about to graze everything into sight, not making more attention about the true from the false. The bitterness comes at their side as surprise, then notifies 'em they were wrong to believe fantasies. In the troubles they are striving to cotton on and to give a meaning 'bout their situation.

Such a situation has incited the noble souls and with virtue to be convinced that this life is no longer what they believed. Some of them are hardly shocked, but are just disappointed to be in this era of self-destruction. Noble souls are lost in a world of mess, values gone, cuz virtues mores got annihilated. None breaking point which may incite the human's spirit to break connection with Beelzebub. Human being desecrates values, most of them are behaving unworthily; a behavior that an animal haint. The animals behave with instinct; the animal behaves better than most humans nowadays, different from the human being who has the instinct, the discernment and the decency notions.

It cannot think, or to understand things; but humans can then does not deserve. We are wondering how to get free from these constant torments, which means succeed honestly without violate the rules of the Almighty.

Some people have success in some illegal deals; they said, one life to live it's hard to be positive. What person to trust in this sadistic world? Thy friends can turn worst enemy tomorrow for personal purposes.

This world faces plight, then most of those who had a noble spirit abandoned their integrity in achieving some rituals banned by the Almighty. This whole panic was engendered by a strange fear, the one do not being attacked in an unexpected or inexplicable way. These practices are spooky, and should be about being eradicated. In reliance on the holy words of God, certain practices are synonym of divine punishment.

The human being has been warned of a world that will emerge soon; even if these words seem distant before human's eyes. They must take it in consideration, as if that revelation will be soon in emersion. There is no greater and saint protector than God, who created then gave enormous advantages to humans being, who must cultivate it throughout their existence. Even if this world is in distress, be aware that God is watching. The greatest asset that he has given us to purify ourselves day by day is the mental strength and the faith.

These sentences are sufficient and positive, if they are interpreted correctly to confront the enemy. In this new era succeed is a thing, but get o' there without being involved in some scandals is something else. Some people are trying to prove who they really are within the worldly; some folks with significant professional situation became callous nowadays. At the same time launched superiority message toward have-nots. Behavior from em uttered, havenots will eat at their fill someday, when they will be competitive to face-up financial plight; a done message to raise aversion.

Several spots in worldwide, numerous folks strive to get easily dough, but often that wampum is a booty. The plight came there then sent its ability to put psychosis of distress, then inculcated them the cult of cheating and fear. From dense psychosis, the extreme manipulation took place then peeps are resolute to launch into easy and fatest ways that life hid the no positive termination. Bystander is the advised demeanor for the foxiest, cuz you will encounter judicial prosecutions, when you dare the judicial system. The judicial system can easily shatter a life in a simple move, if you ain't in the same league.

Peeps who have the clouts can hardly out from there, tied with irreversible reputation, if suspicion topical. Frailer minds misbehaving, noxious deeds handled as pastime by their clique. Dire deeds versus hard-up people, snaffling their livelihood and waylaying 'em been noticed by antagonits. . We really live of kind; mercy toward the person beside is archaic. Outliving till offence is the trend, lack of stamina does not work in such society. When you got your pathos dominant, you will be regarded by everyone as being a Sula bassana. They became hard and fast since an irrational angst came troubled their sense.

Feeble minded turned as marginal, incessant fails blown wide open their lack of faith and assurance. They sank in evil. Live in such plight became a millstone, be a breadwinner ain't suitable for. Go getter turned as first sufferer of such system. Most of us became doomladen, bananas and bottled-up. That is not a fast one; iterative observance gave us such hint. Standoffish we are too, behave wickedly most of them espoused, put hindrance is the purpose of such attitude. Mayhem, strain and dense poverty set a total mess in minds, but not spare so a world in total perdition.

Poverty been drawn for a category of persons, but another reality in resistance came into sight then made several victims in the bourgeoisie's clan. Misery absorbs the world gradually. No terrific ambiance that left moneyed people with no alternative. An only issue been softly advised at their side, the one to have a genuine and secured whereabouts. Flee towards gated community was the idea of their respective lackey, being racy became hazardous for itself even. Get a look toward these upstarts who strive to reach the uptowns.

To evidence they are in the beat, is the first purpose of such move. Survival instinct turned as one of negative facets of several characters. Nothing to lose till their dying day became motto, if despair knocks behind the door. A strategic moment, for the Old Nick achieves his dirty work on 'em. When misery appears someplace, it comes with its destructives luggages. Kinda luggage identified as debauchery, illnesses, trafficking and corruption. Always when it leaves, chaos and degradation of mores appear, so it strictly hands some irreversible sequels to dwellers. Kinda dwellers will face critical sequences to out head from daily troubles.

That genuine mental suffering turned most of em as symbol of the negativity. A Minority cyann sense that dense unease, to be made of money is their current shelter. But others form of concerns come at their side to ruin progressively their shangri-la. Even they are racy, the thing turns of kind to teach nobody lives without problems. God is the only one who can save peeps from ambient pauperization. Through these terrible and sad events most of people think, they will find the peace in the indifference.

A risky bet, cuz never there will have a little peace, if there is always misery's face before peeps' eyes. Although they peer, several fellow citizens don't able to cotton on the sense of this word (humble). Our era witnessed most of world citizens are more gifted to razzle-dazzle, than trying to figure out the meaning of our coming here. Life is done to learn then decrypt signs to avoid hazardous situation where can find ourselves trapped. Learn everyday cuz of incessant situations, despite never you will get the picture of world's system. Only the master can easily goes trough it.

Some people kindle to flaunt their means before the eyes of anybody, for getting praises from flunkies. Most of us need to alter their mindset, for better advancing the world. A minority ain't feeling the world of vexations, cuz kinda trepidations ain't pertain em, or try to put us into the trap of appearrances. A rumor been shouted, they are rich since their first breath, by their kinfolks or by their trade. Misery they never face it, for in relishing the charisma and the lure. If gossips are real, so I ain't wish you to go facing the world of anxiety, cuz that can be twice time more arduous for you than us. You can cought kinda people into some idiot behaviors, idiot behaviors that anytime ruin their life, by lack of perspective.

Overhelmed when you hear kinda history, God saves them from major concerns, but they put themselves into a negative situation. Only people who are inside this bitter trouble can testify what they are seeing. We wont to 'bout kinda feeling, cuz my homeland born core this struggle. 2 kinda middle-classes have been noticed following zones.

First category is people who came straight from wretchedness, and who haven't need that somebody expounds them the over there's reality. Kinda peeps tholed before to be well-to-do. Peeps oversee poverty's motion, for not facing avoidable slip-up. Throw money down the drain does not appear in their respective mindset.   It is in the interest of everyone to proceed of kind nowadays; cuz bitter bathos can come into sight. Entrapped into a negative wind, a boob can be irreversible. Fatal for your integrity, if your mind is ain't inured. Misery gaining ground each coming day then its course of action tips us off then sent its ability to trash. You could count on close parents or cronies. Nowadays the plight blown wide opens another reality. Data have been upset the apple cart. Cuz your own struggle against problems, you will be alone to deal with its stinky lure.

Every man for himself; peeps who could lend you a hand in back days, when time was not critical are trying to survive at the other side. If you think that someone can give you an honorable way out without distraught feeling, you become nutcase.

Only God ablest to help someone without this history outs from another mouth. We all need going for broke to have stamina then to become mindful towards life's traps. Dark side of the life is unavoidably qualified as babylon by wise peeps, a value judgment only based on their doings. Life became delusive then tied with beatitude and evil fortune. Its side the more fearsome is, it canalizes easily people's mind and sink em at despair swiftly. Stay safe, if you wanna outlast in this lost struggle. A lost struggle since the start of the humanity, that seems that everything been already penned.

Land; where many of our fellow citizens kicked the bucket tragically. Some peeps are struggling with their destiny, not knowing where to find the good recipe for an unconvincing narrow escape. Problems at every door then peeps don't know which way to turn. Nobody can ratify a genuine explanation. Some of us can notify, it comes from everywhere, whilst oafs think woe will strike elsewhere and their good fortune will last forever.

Wait being in constant throe. You will hit the ceiling, thinking never you will escape from iterative jigsaw. Time that your mind turns inefficient then leads you often into indescribable occurrences. Reckon on to face hardships, ordeals averred as horrendous, cuz are too far to be trouble-free for several minds. Strong stamina work required, before to sink at despair swiftly, or being interned in nuthouse. During this, well-mannered people will have a pity thought for you. During the mercy of wise people, your foes will celebrate their dark victory. They have the unexpected chance to deride you before people's eyes, chiefly if you had achievement and the esteem of some people.

The plight is in a cleft stick, few faithful people keep on to reiterate an absolute confidence without rear thinking to the Supreme Being. Scarce are some people who continue to keep this worthy mindset. Only some of em can give you the genuine definition of the galley. They keep the head up, despite probs. Fed up, most of world citizens chosen dark side of life, by the same banter their faith with devil's contract.

Human being is a thick mystery then is versatile. God gave the success key at some persons who could solve tribulations that this world encounters. But some of these leaders confiscated all monetary funds, use it as they want. Another irresponsible behavior been noticed at their side. Cuz they don't respect knowledge that God gave them to rule with fairness. Their manner to proceed is scandalous for some people and a normal behavior for profiteers. The most eye catching demeanor is, there are some peeps who ain't agree with kinda unfairness, and could change trajectory when next session topical, without embarrassment. This band of idiots is the adepts of transhumance.

Some among peeps are reliable, cuz they espoused the values that God instituted. We often noticed that the first move of a human being is he cares 'bout him, before to assist someone.   Even if his neighbor is in the need, he will be leading by his survival instinct. New trends or the human nature imposes him to proceed of kind.

When you solicit some persons to assist someone, they often disallow, relating to you their early stinky files to relieve their conscience. Even the request is feasible. He often refuses, advising you to care 'bout that daily stinky challenge in front; a navel-gazing instituted by destitution; an attitude that turned as appalling custom. Most of peeps proceed of kind by lack of humanism. The few remaining proceed of kind, cuz are exceeded by that stinky plight. Nowadays request kinda services to some folks, turned as the drink sea. Hard is to meet a man of God and it is not easy to be a man of God.

To be a man of God emanates straight of God's bestowment; a donation that God gives to his servant according his tolerance degree. Someday you can meet a man of God, who accepts to achieve this gesture, cuz a man of God does not falter, when it about to help his neighbor. He only does this by humanism, and then a voice will assured him, that he can encounter same baptism of fire someday. What you will be, alone in a dark without rope of salvage?

Scarce are men of God, cuz 95 percent of people are picturing an eventual lack of recognition. It's why they eye up the good outlook is to forgo the challenge. Most of people who asserted being men of God have a rear thinking, when comes the time to give a leg up the neighbor. What tell about another mental-makeup, peeps who lend a hand foxily? They befriend those who will earn them a benefit, just to earn something more attractive in return. When you have a little chance for a vindication about kinda wariness, kinda folks argue, life turned in tricky challenge.

They all stated everyone must care about him, without being affected by events behind. Cuz when they were in the need, nobody wanted help them, and nobody been close to them. It's why they have no remorse to proceed of kind. Wise people in the world can have sadness about fairness. Cuz it seems that the fairness has never been instituted by human being in the world. Perhaps their foxiness had not reach this level, it's why the result ain't surprised mindful people.

Several persons in the world have no initiation about fairness. Numerous persons have no percept 'bout this value, cuz this did not include in their education. Either their parents ignored these virtues, or either they had not boldness or the time to inculcate these principles to children. According some people, often person you help, will betray you. We're agreeing if you helped him, in waiting something in return. Cuz when you help for something, you will be often disappointed. Cuz few persons are thankful nowadays. 'Bout this kinda topic, people have their own clue, cuz it is not an accurate science. Some people gotta make-out that the fairness have always a positive termination.

Opposite the unfairness is of same kind that the nastiness. And those 2 words have never brought a positive upshot. Don't be amazed, if the thing turned in castigation beyond and here.

In blackmail we recognize the worthy human-being, in troubles and difficulties, we recognize the genuine men. Which does not mean that these real men ain't shown mental weakness in their route sometimes, when shitty ordeals been before their eyes. A real man is not the one who is talkative, but the one who has the solid capacity to face up hard ordeals of life, in resolving them one by one in silence. Why be baddie? Be wicked emanates from nonsense. Whether you wanna yes or no, someday you will beg a help from others, cuz only God is to shelter from everything. A trivial ordeal and you can hit the ceiling. Without the help of some people you will bite the dust.

And worst someday you can kneel down in begging an amicable solution, when despair knocks at your door. Cuz a human being is nothing, despite all ranks that he can have in that society. It's why human-being gotta be brought-up with anyone, even things move positively at his side. A positive step then your way will be quiet here and beyond. Even having annoyance, never mind about it. Cuz the solace and the relief are beyond.

Nowadays mindful folks can see the life of people gonna toward a disaster. Several people see powerlessly their life takes an eerie bustle. Cuz nowadays nothing holds long, even things which are down to earth. Cuz even if they repugn that, the human-being is in the elementary state of the life, whether he wants yes or no. Despite knowledge he can have, and all the developments that we have gotten. We sustain this according their manner to think and their manner to proceed, when they have a little power or responsibility on peeps. (An intelligent person, who is no elementary in perception, always he will coy. Cuz figured-out his means ain't issued from his own ingenuity.

But of an unreadable science above him, ain't detectable for naked eyes, so 'bout that you are not maven. You can feel the despondency of people; they have qualms to fall into woe. Cuz make-out kinda disillusionment can turn in nightmare. Most of people have no mercy; life is difficult if God does not intervene.

When you ask to people about the troubles they often encounter, you will underline that their mind-set are opposed, even they seem going in same way in appearance. You will see that some persons don't know how to proceed in this brainteaser. Nobody knows where stepping, cuz everywhere in worldwide there are troubles of all kinds. Numerous persons don't unravel what happening to them. Most of them don't figure-out, they floating in shark's ocean. All these folks, who argue on the topic, have same perceptual experience.

A classic struggle which became a pet fancy then seems a lost struggle; tight till nobody is able to deal against. But this does not avert when they confab on the topic, you can see everyone between them strive to head this public debate. Often kinda discussion brings disputes, if some among them haven't pull in to gain recognition. Most of em think that he mastered in knowledge, difficulties that the world facing. Sometimes peeps whine, hit the ceiling instead of give him a backup. People beside them whispered he ain't godly.

They consigned to oblivion, sometimes some desponded persons have needed to wipe out from his brain some hardships. It's why he does jeremiad, as though it has been said that life will be easy-going. A human who leads a daily struggle must be complimented concerning his self-abnegation. Life became a real chore for go-getter. With his self-denial, the human being will swallows down with difficulty that a harmful thing comes to dash his nisus; especially if he is law abiding-citizen. That's why the most feeble minded have decreased faith. We also noticed there is ordeal and beside this, there is shitty hardship from high troubles, where you risk losing your nous.

Logically a human being who suffered a hardship, hit the ceiling most of time by cowardice. Cuz no problem is compatible with poor human's mind. If you have a say, don't be a Janus-faced, neither talk through your hat, just turn out what you experienced in your legendary route. Only a genuine faith can push someone do not sink totally in despair. Cuz with an authentic faith, the shock will be at 50% of its capacity.

How many people cling up in a genuine faith nowadays? There are some people who are in current failures at all levels and their minds yield to the amentia. Wrong people took the world in hostage. Wrong behavior brought psychos. Peeps found themselves trapped in a grip of fear, modern barbarism turned as most logical cause. All this is characterized, by the treachery and awful deeds committed by half-wits who endorse the dark empire. Peeps are ready to put you into deep, just to abscond from a plight.

So stay safe, most of em only have interests. Mainly when you get stranded; you will see them in real traitor. The toast of life is naturally the success, but in first you must be able to hang yourself in this achievement. The success became an utter torment for knowledge holders. The success can be bitter, following ordeals you face up before to get it. In some levels the life becomes elusive by its odd involution. Only in the future, you will catch sight your slip-up, a predicament that will make your life pernicious. Plainly your life risks being destructive, if you ain't restrain yourself.

That's the end, and anybody gotta take a sense of right, that's the end. The countdown is in motion since the first sign. The beginning of human's decline is started by disrepair. Most of people can't see this upheaval is coming soon, above our heads as the Damocles' sword. Violence, cheating, murders and suicides; the list of negative deeds spreads. From there emerged some human's facets, that we don't dare fumble. Life is no more terrific, news on telly became negative, and the idiot-box became an instrument of negative deeds and manipulation A real shitty mess without expound dirty pending files that most of people turned a blind eye.

Most of people became wretched, even their gait show another thing. Don't let them fool you; 90% of minds are in the grip of life. First signs of decline are unbearable for worthy people, cuz life is into infernal cycle, and the trap of appearances became large. God's science deposed us at this level, its unlimited capability to appraise kinda jeopardy.

Where, the human being sinks by limited knowledge. The flunkies' sect is gaining ground, cuz of pauperization. Their mindset advised them the art of fake subservience. How many people repugn God's choices, if choices do not gonna to the same wavelength. Yet these faithful men blazon-out to be men of God. Their lack of longanimity makes their faith impure, as they pretend the opposite? Or it's just straits times? A sin is a sin. Only God knows if this doubt propels them in impure side of life. Cuz only God got the ability.

Anyway people don't see eye to eye. Each day most of peeps act-up, and wise kin group sees in em immaturity. No human's mind is efficient to cotton on God's options and God's knowledge, without to get bogged down into some deets. First off we're simple humans, with none rank of upper knowledge. Accordingly we ain't having the knowledge and the grey-matter to figure-out God's science, his criteria before acting. Stay safe, therefore you run the risk to turn loco.

If you try to get God, chiefly in the wrong way, always you will sink into wrong end of the stick. The only way to hold him in awe been noticed, a way emerged from a flawless faith. Don't ever forget that the world is not a level playing field. You will figure-out it the crack of doom, when your eyes are staring veracity of divine tidings. Most of them think to be able handling everything. So confident their mental makeup assured 'em, they can pass trough an absolute darkness without troubles. But the Supreme Being led 'em where kinda boldness gets end.

Everyplace is same concerning the inquisitiveness and the malevolence. At this time of life, the all mighty schooled us, we are equal, cuz same harmful symptoms in us. Positive mores and these humans' shortcomings are classified according their reach through the world. All over the world, you will encounter these 2 ineluctable sides of life. Most of heads favor the warfare than to lose their power, they have no acquaintance, but only self-seeking as foxy people noticed.

Their way to rule drove in despair have-nots, cuz the new system that they enforced weighted in favor of the wealthy peeps. Just the addled-head abide to be governed by hatred and by ruffianism, instead of stick together. Most of real villains are in the upper crust, and they are watching with a superiority sense, whilst imbeciles carry a spooky panic stricken in the world towns.

You've given them a stick to beat you, so don't kvetch. We go rack and ruin, and it will be chilling for each flesh. There will no heartsease, if things move of kind, its eye catching. Some God-fearing men have an aversion of this frame of mind, whilst some peeps conceive the hatred of. The society sired its own foes by its outlook tied with a constant discrimination. Some spots in the world are often ruled by featherbrained, it's why the new society has a callow air, just an ascertained occurrences. In an increasing degree, we will face-up yahoos, who will come to psych us. They lay down the law nowadays.

Gats give willies anymore; and folks don't falter to shrug, when they gun someone down, whatever contentious. They achieve that deed to corroborate that they are dreadful mobster. Unconsciousness or they've gotten the fallen angel within the mind. They are anymore law-abiding citizen, try to hinder them could be a never-ending seeing-red. Nobody is pugnacious; there are more overriding topics, the search of knowledge for instance, instead of idle away to throw his weight around. Life has anymore meaning with that booming dirtiness, for peeps who try to unscramble the sense of all that mess.

This epoch is so odd and tricky that you risk puffing the sens (in life, it could go either way). Never human's conception will make-out this far-out side of life, cuz nobody can appraise its flight. People turned a blind eye to the modern barbarism, by a dread of retaliatory. The genuine Shangri-La is too far from us, and the only option will be God whether you wanna yes or no. Go toward your creator in due course.

Bear in mind, that to follow God, request to be a genuine soldier in the soul, cuz devil's acolytes constantly in the struggle. Hallucinating, don't be astounded to run into folks with mind full of demons. Cuz you are downright in their glorious era. Only the no mindful does not reckon with it. That's just the harmful effects of the era 666's mindset. If we were sure that our religious conception is flawless, to the key the felicity, most of God-fearing men will be enticed to rejoin God swiftly. (In the case that God had legalized the suicide, they gladly risk it).

Cuz often their whole world shattered by these detrimental data. Some peeps preach veracity straight from holy credence, but often behave in the manner contrary. Short timeout to realize they were out from God's path. They don't dare to natter 'bout it, alongside talkative folks. People have afraid of people's opinions than God's insight. I don't mean the poor wench, but opposite the broke fella in first, even women face troubles of same kind.

Often the poor male is the one who often meets treachery in modern times, following ordeals that he will encounter. And also, who can profit following subjects, following occasions that he'll has. Relations between men and women are tense then often originate serious bones of contention, if the materialism leads the relation. Some people think they are better than other fellow citizens. First deception noticed at their side, when they came across us. We blown wide open to them that we don't care 'bout drongo mentality. People who have dosh try fiercely to rise up their account, has the more reason the have-nots.

Look at in gambling hell, where each day the righteous God gave them breath. Numerous people fork-out money foolishly, just for hoping to have something more stirring. They often squander bread, without dither. During this misuse the down and out peeps outliving before God's eyes; where is the spirit of compassion? During that time have-nots are musing to alight in the street to face leaders.

Financier troubles, dubiousness, pauperization, unemployment above their heads as Damocles' sword. Situation that incited them to launch a long and risky struggle. Struggle that often turns the involved govt oppressor. They don't have a seemly life; all these protests march are done by fear to become the prey of the society. No leader care about, most of these demonstrations remain without positive outcome, often told-off harshly by involved govt.

Some people sustain they have a picture 'bout people who splurge through famous areas overtime and out of view of nosey, in stead of fulfil duties. Often kinda veiled revelation can turn in blackmail. We have no substantiation 'bout it, even some hints are coming to us. Kinda system can obscure your life, if you ferret out the sensible files. When your steps go against Babylon's system, retaliations will come into sight, according the file you call forth. At some levels the shaped system is very hush-hush then can easily destroys a life.

There are people in that society that you can't confront face to face without troubles. They are highly protected by that system that they created. At the other side, your so called leaders shield some persons high you can't ideate. That system they engendered, in the long run works reverse. Do not create you mare's nest; you are just a little tile in that vicious game of manipulation. Don't niggle, don't mind about this rip off, cuz they are misleading in God's eyes. This kind of sit-in did by madden folks are often treated by persons who do not care about their tribulations; it's why often the outcome is not positive.

Or if demonstrators have the happiness that the quest becomes positive, often kinda files can take a considerable time, considerable time to dissuade next claimers. They don't want the progress for have-nots. In the other side some folks, who got the clout are helped swiftly, when they requested something. Life spares nobody, it moves and throwing jinx on ill-fated humans. The death appears as fair umpire to remember to peeps there is someone supreme.

No nepotism, you can intellect God's hands in it. Shit-stirrers who hatch frictions stand so far from essential. Ill-will that can embroil in negative situation before their eyes, in the long run. They throw around their weight to prove something before some peeps' eyes, who discreetly rate 'em as oafish. These weirdoes missed the plot.

They fathom nothing as they have no history. Don't be tempted to engender a situation that risks exceeding you negatively in the long run. When you raise an action, hope this deed ain't turn in negative. This deed will bumps into you, whether positive or negative. Wretched time where you will come down in the world, you will spot that you reckon without your host.

Life got precepts, precepts that peeps contravene without vacillate, and the ban turned in major pastime. Most of peeps stare all their means and hope sagging. Impotent to face this muck up, numerous amongst them became hobo. Kinda upheavals throw most of em in suicide.

These suicides hide unholy histories. Most of time we engender unconsciously our own decline, kinda instability that bares its extreme aspect. The suicide is unspeakable, and will remain always ineffable. Involved persons in these tragedies shoulda ken nothing is definitive. Nothing is conclusive. You can face iterative bummy of days, then the following day God deles all these concerns from your suffered mind. Your nous can egg you on to wonder 'bout the genuine dialectics of all these far-out occurrences. Ordeal or not ordeal, peeps' brain melts down. Trying to ferret out the provenience, presto we about face in the starting point, as if we never left this fact finding level.

We draw a blank then gleaned from this curio, these supervened happenings should fall out; why, we don't know. After this lost innocence, we straight call it quits, then toyed why the perception "Supreme Being". My clan assured don't walking blind, before to get lost in this cryptic landscape. We are stating 'bout kinda evil chance, as if we have whelmed our fuss.

But we ain't ineffectual to cognize, how we shall give up the ghost and the manner the ruin of us will appear. A hint actuated some of us, to muse some kismet been traced out. A concept jettisoned by sceptics, even substantiate about it turn most of 'em edgy. Even some hardships seem being traced out, to think each episode is linked turned some peeps in foolhardy.

Easy going far from God's instructions, sometimes responsible of our deeds we are, even things ain't seem eased off. Heard some of 'em apprised that the end will be pain free; we can't head into this dimension, cuz thick closed book in it. A thing is sure from doubt, heaven really hard to find, but inferno ain't hard to find. Everyone must inure himself for the final hardship. Peeps diss the Supreme Being by daily unethical deeds; the taciturnity is an odd feedback. Denuded of savvy culprits virtually sink into jahannam. God is angry then blows wide open his insight 'bout our misconducts.

God defines his outlook by whammies. Look around you how the poverty is powerful, each coming day with is pile of anathemas and trials. Some peeps go ballistic, striving to picture the trigger of such mayhems. Sorry, response before your eyes. I really cotton on, why wise peeps assured that God has an infinite leniency. If God goes for an eye for an eye, a tooth for a tooth, never humans will last a minute in the world. They will be decimating by their own deeds, cuz negative air will incur a terrible God's wrath, a lack of brainpower that will be the synonym of the rude awaken. Can you bear out his existence, question from atheists.

God-fearing men answered them; are you able to spot the air that you are breathing; or to grab the air although you know its veracity? Don't endeavor to draw a comparison between the beliefs. You cyann draw our credence off, therefore a drawn out debate wil be topical. Believe in God does not mean monkey around. Noisy and unpleasant are the original aspects of humans. Our eyes noticed an infernal outliving.

As if God flung them the first wind of castigation. Most of peeps are no longer confidently according all that turn of phrase. A question riles some peeps, is a day they will break loose from this whirlwind of despair that some of 'em deliberately hatched? Most of 'em minded that life became long faced, and stirs into a huge minus factor.   It ain't a pretty sight for people who brood about this finding.

Positive virtues deleted by evil's ringleaders, they sent diabolic challenge for coming generations. Their struggle will be under a continuum aspect then seems being eased off for firebrands. The continuum is not controllable; it will cause the ruin of 'em in the first approach. The legacy of great parents ebbing, the trigger of it, is pioneers of worldly. The world is gazette beside some peeps, "Succeed our die", while another category of person yowl "succeed or succeed". Some of them are cold as the devil, when they wanna keep a hindrance out. The Old-Nick coaxed 'em for a so called primacy, but some of 'em ain't picture terms of kinda contract.

Supremacy tied with indescribable sacrifices. The human-being who rules with assaultive behavior, will disappear with kinda belief. The human who puts his hopes in Old Nick's hands, will find the ephemeral success and dupery in the palm of this one, then the jahannam in the other palm. Aftermaths their minds don't know, and then gladly risk their soul integrity. Fatal misconception, if the stake echoed a kind of paramountcy. The Old-Nick came straight to us to lift the tantalization. You will cotton on, when you figured out that the tantalization was ignis retuus; being the fall guy after years of alliance, time for the Supreme Being to appear for every dereliction of duty. A terrible meeting.

Some of us got a conundrum rattling through their mind, why God does not sear these fallen angels. The devil risen a perverse and pernicious kingdom, and then sent several acolytes toward a hellish quest of soul. God is God; it is not our role to have kinda clarification, wise peeps shouted confidently.

The Old-Nick scrutinized closely, then figured out that effective way to affect humans is to form hybrid with human race. We all shouting the Old-Nick is really powerful, but consigned to oblivion that we are the trigger. Peeps who are trapped into whirlwind of despair are barfing criticisms all around, and monished a probable aftermaths, as we early said. Countless folks have no domesticity, only the work, "just to earn their keep", but this does not avert most of 'em encountered concerns of all kinds.

There are several persons ready to die sooner than to have kinda life. Cuz they haven't guts to face up the negative routine. People who birth through troubles can face it, but often with predicament, cuz they used to. But in these orations misery is showing to us another reality, which is its capability to spit up terrible sequels (gloominess, mores degradation etc....... Nowadays numerous people in worldwide have guts to gall their govt. According them the governments don't carry out their task.

On account kinda negligence pauperization gaining ground, are you agree with their conception? Through seethe situation numerous governments are the target of some revolutionists, often came from of deprived areas; these radical persons evidence, they scunnered. They are demonstrating a fierce aggro to put down the hegemony of which they don't leverage. Again have-nots are bugged and dare shouting out at everyplace, showing their wired do not being included among considerable persons. And not to mention the shabbiness they are constrained to stomach in an absolute hush.

They get stranded and treading crossly in streets. In front of this busts that can be very hazardous. The implicated govt strives to achieve efficient talks. It's a modus operandi to abate that insurrection, but often they can't call the shots, cuz peeps already have the jitters. Often contention propels involved peeps in red mist, and vehement termination becomes the only issue. The involved state is often narked by demonstrators, and often purpose to consign constables in riot zone, for restoring the order.

That's o'er there where all frays started, because 90% of times, when cops come in the area the scuffle become unavoidable. None of the 2 camps wanna surrender in first for asserting his rights. Often you can clap eyes on how some cops hit the ceiling, behaving negatively. Look like as a fiend when they have a step to achieve, cuz they ain't waver to give a fierce drubbing to some persons who hamper their say-so.

What tell about marchers who often lose their sang-froid, in yielding to enormity? Just to evidence to cops, they ain't get the wind up by their so called attendance. You can gaze at, it's the same modus-operandi through the world. World citizens and coppers became cowboys in the world streets; we are not in the far-west. With social networks, they all bust a gut just to evidence something to adverse camp. Overtime after these contests, you can be all ears that some citizens revile the cops or start to abhor them. We mustn't dismiss from our mind, annihilate strife is cop's task. Often outcomes can be awful in some countries, cuz if it was 'bout cops often we heard there were injured.

But nowadays it became as army operation, cuz bloodshed on rendezvous. Nevertheless in front of these busts, there are numerous cops who misapply their power, power that constitution allocates 'em. Stepping over the rule of thumb, they shoulda not dare to cut across. Often these harmful deeds are achieved by some constables, cuz their only incentive is the hard feeling. A grudge that they have gotten, cuz most of world citizens ain't stand in awe of the police constable. Anyway most of people apply their posture to make bold, when some representatives hand them a little ascendancy. People are no longer fear of a rozzer.

There is no longer respect toward the uniform, cuz most of people have not latched on the meaning of the word respect. According some people, the spite that some coppers demonstrate during their interventions has a definition. A definition which means before they become a bizzy, they have good deal suffered by people deportment. And it's just a sort of return match for them to be cop, and being above troublesome citizens, they could not face up before.

They added that kinda cops hope to encounter peeps they consider as punks, when they are in patrol, just to peeve them. Bad habits deeply ingrained in the society. They define it as unexpected occasion to rebuke them, when they stumble into the guile. If a constable plans a situation for assuaging his envy, in the only purpose to assert him, he does not know his duty assignment. You can descry them water down, when they strip down cop's uniform. They are obliged to behave of kind for not encountering a counterstroke from intractable peeps.

When a cop has not the uniform, the risk swells for him if he is reconnoitred by wrongdoers. You can eye dutiful coppers hit the ceiling, according people who behave as the skyjackers; often out of view they unexpectedly blow their top. You can observe 'em sometime after have whelmed someone with cuffs; they often keep on to cosh him. Cops drop a clanger, after this lack of lucidity or excessive temper, the eyewitness will be perceived as persona non grata.

According pious minds the damaging things that some amongst us practicing as usual behavior drove us in this filthy plight. And added they got suspicion that nowadays God looking at us crossing his arms. 'Bout this matter some people acquiescing, and for others kinda utter are far-fetched history. We are living in a profligate world, where most of persons became wantons, increasing the profligacy in all its bearings. The foul play is soaring; most of people have ungodliness through a world in disorder.

These unbearable behaviors were noticed, tied with muddled thinking and economic chaos that numerous world citizens are familiarized. The harmful attitude runs up with astonishing pace. Several folks have free agent; the word taboo is no longer took stock of in their vocab. And natter 'bout lechery topics became a current talks; the sex and the age don't matter. Opposite if you don't hold with kinda state of mind, "you are as thick as two planks", it is topical. Don't be bowl over, cuz the world is backwards.

Most of people wanna succeeding, for most of them the goal is to have dough, wipe off dirties concerns and getting the reverence from other persons. A normal attitude according most of moods, musing that's only there they will have an honorable way out. This does not remain the primordial thing for the few remaining people. After this, motivations diverged following people; we have not the same nurture. For some folks the incentive is to be fine, and also to avail the drudges. In the other side where the motivation is of no avail, just to have wampum and marvel at the cocottes, then to be on a spree.

This negative stance is the result of a past, where it seemed they have a great deal endured. Most of folks want to be nouveau riche then step into parvenus' clan. Kinda mindset prods them to muse they gonna made up the lost time. Wise people assured never they shall make up the lost time; affirmation based on early events. Some of them are keened to get more funds, for being reverenced in this consumer society.

An imbecilic mindset motivated by a maturity deficiency; odd mindset, just to have people at his mercy. Numerous people became uppity, when they have a reaching; they are incapable to restrain themselves. Everything they can reflect for others know 'bout their reaching, they will achieve it without embarrassment. Kinda state of mind is increasing; and became a normal attitude according some peeps' belief.

You can hear most of them assured, when someone is moneyed, he gotta turn a blind eye then apply every man for himself. They told if peeps were in the same stance, they will proceed of kind. Take luxury things, flaunt before the eyes of anybody, and added youth must have its fling. Kinda attitude is divisive; we can't go through. What people don't have the guts to do in the past; they achieve it without falter, but can't bewilder experienced people. As some people understood, there are numerous people who are ready to be up there with the leaders, till gainsaying the Supreme Being. How many people have been killed, for money, success and lot of silly things, alone God knows the figures.

Nice citizens cannot breathe these stink files of some cowards, but well-kept in fresh by the Great Spirit, just for the judgment day; awful deeds done for being a man of means. It isn't good to begrudge someone that you don't picture the provenance of his achievement. Numerous people yield in front of temptations of life, when it 'bout cash. Kinda peeps think lolly will be scant then most of them became corrupted. Money is destructive, and most of people are inefficient to face it worthily. Peeps sustained a rumor; dosh doesn't achieve everything. But each passed day bear out this trend is false, then notified by all clans. People's speeches are bogus, life is hard and nobody can't afford. Rear these speeches are veiled odd practices.

Peeps are complaining all time about life, about weather, about everything. But this does not prevent them to stand everywhere with valuable things and with good health. During that time there are peeps who are under a constant threat of war and bombardment. These ones have no life and don't able to describe what looks like the peace.

There are people who really suffer, and others who haven't this kinda trouble for now. But nevertheless amongst these people there are some persons who try to have gain from the system. Peeps who alleged to suffer to swindle easy preys or from some organizations, and those who feign to have strong situation just to gouge them. This plight brought numerous persons to be wary, and bottled up.

Nowadays the problem is, who is who?. Who tells the truth, or who doesn't mean it, and this behavior to be bottled became very overriding for anybody among us. Cuz nowadays this remains the only way, to escape from cheating which is orchestrated by wrongdoers. Even people who are swindler proceed of kind, cuz as anybody in the world; a hustler doesn't crave someone hustling him. Numerous of our fellow citizens suffered, numerous amongst them sympathize with Heineken or Campbell-clan became polluted and often joined hobo's clan. Always instead of give them a hand, for that they find a probable way out.

Some persons like seeing people in the need to have a superiority sense. They only able to judge negatively, a thing that seems became trivial. When these situations befallen you can see a kinda indifference from people. Some peeps are foolishly thinking, these unhappiest victims of this worldly are scoundrels, and don't have contribution in the society. What kinda society we are talking 'bout, individualist and stinky society. A society that does not worth something, devalued by its inhabitants. Stated rudeness, thinking they are interesting; till whisper these ones don't deserve to be helped. Kinda persons are in the soup and they need to get up to cope, instead of staying in all corners driving to beg, ya ears can hear..

Rude statement, drongo mentality are ingrained custom in 'em. Some people talk rudely 'bout others that they don't found an interest. Many people became undisciplined and whimsical, everyplace they gonna, they move with this harmful attitude as if their parents don't educate em. You can view inside stadiums, the violence done by some onlookers.

Often when anthems are passing, some airheads jeer against the opposing nation that they qualified as opponents, by lack of education. The sport became a suitable scope, for some shit stirrers to unveil their lack of education and the dirty odium concealed in 'em. Often you can hear some persons get out from their mouths score of discriminatory words, cuz it's the best place for being unleashed. These hoodlums don't hide themselves, when they proceed. The goal is to achieve a drongo game, and showing they are hard bitten.

Some sports are anymore restful games, especially in football. Often you can meet a sort of violence. The occasional violence; when your team is in trip towards another town. Often it's over there; you will hear numerous players who are insulted, and not to mention the constant strain between onlookers. Cuz they belong to the adverse team. The contentious is straight forgotten, if an adverse player signs a contract in their club. At this moment never you will hear kinda incidents, where he has been insulted. No hate is shown toward him, now he defends the interest of the football club.

The sport became clan deals. Sometimes we witness some peeps expulsed from their flat. Kinda persons have a difficulty to pay their rent; then receive a formal notice to put em under pressure. The formal notice rudely invites them to leave, cuz they are a defaulter. Often some furious tenants profit about delay, to obliterate the flat just by injustice sentiment, prior to leave the accommodation. Often these persons mean they have been duped by their bank that propose 'em those flats, it's why they backfire against them.

At the other side, there are people who have private lodgings. Some among them decide to wait cops to face em diplomatically. But don't take initiative to damage their flat by reprisals. Often their refusal to leave the house on time brings confrontations between expelled persons and cops. Often it's their advisers, who advise them to stay at home until expulsion. This allows them to have a little time to build a defence. There are people, who got always a little hope to keep on dwelling at home, and their problem gonna be solved. Wait cops, till they request them to relinquish.

Expelled persons abandon the flat without confrontation, but also with regrets and several questions in abeyance. How they gonna solve a such problem. Some among them are realist, cuz they leave in the delay, before the cops humiliate them. Even they haven't the way out; they proceed of kind to keep their self-esteem and pride. Going to work became an assault course, for those who have the privilege to have an activity.

And ain't consign to oblivion this enquires several exertions, cuz earn his living became tiring in this infernal era. During that time that some citizens are trying to be a go getter, other persons are achieving trick confidence to bring at home, just to feed their families. In some areas people don't eat correctly. It is t not everyday that kinda peeps eat at their fill; the presence of money dearth is dense at their side. Kinda persons are brave and deserve an absolute respect.   Most of em manifest a flawless dignity. A dignity that some persons who haven't serious problems haint, cuz their names tied with some scandals despite their positive situation.

Lack of respect is noticed toward em came from haughty persons. Haughty persons who have an imbeciclic manner to lead their life. The sentiment of superiority brought the dissents and the hate then veiled the vision of peeps. It is not anybody who deserves the respect; deprived areas or middle class does not matter. Often their doings incited wise peeps to notify things of kind. The Old-nick has his allied in all areas, and has his way to proceed according the zone where his aura is in sight.

Numerous people play the haugthy persons, but they are broke. They can't make ends meet every month, their arrogance is just a sign of hangs-up. There are some worthy persons who request nothing from others; has the more reason to bum something. But no one can read their situation, no complain, no arrogance. They have a solid training about dignity's value. Life schooled us that we can't judge someone without deeply hobnob him.

Even to frequent him, not seems to be sufficient, cuz a human being can turn as devil's son step by step. Inside some slums there are good citizens; intelligent and full of hospitality. Some moneyed peeps don't make the difference between drudges, thinking a hard up, will forever remain a down and out. The bias becomes an infliction, for people who came from suburbs or shantytowns, and then are pointed as molesters. What tell 'bout people who have been badly-off in back days and dwelled inside outskirts?

And today God gave them an opportunity to realize something positive, till they have forgotten their back days, hail criticism on suburbanites. Only reaching can alter peeps in ungrateful, unveiling their genuine character. Most of people forget swiftly elements that constituted their back days. What God already gave, he can get it back in a flash. God does not acquaint, when he decides something. Beguilers are here and handling poverty as means of gain. Tricksters can be a runabout or can to belong to the upper crust.

In this no terrific atmosphere, the trick became compulsory for these cardsharps. Kinda persons have 2 different purposes. Those who came from deprived area proceed for outliving, and those who came from to the upper crust proceed for not losing their standard of life. They don't make difference 'bout poor and rich people. What interesting them, is to have takings from anybody they consider as easy prey.

The social class doesn't matter; these predators are far and wide. Therefore careful, these predators don't have a well definite gait. Up to the present, there are people who endeavor to comprehend the task of government. But nobody grok that, cuz during hustings candidates make pledge overtime right and left. None effective sign, people are watching their situation downgrades. In numerous countries, most of presidents elected ain't done the deal that lot of people expected. Numerous people, who had confidence toward these candidates can't grok these iterative failures.

We have a hunch that nowadays in hustings time, constituents balloted by duty. We peer some of 'em lost the envy 'bout kinda matter, and they withdraw from the scene. Most of 'em cheesed off, agnized same smooth talks 'bout govt bill, when they are all ears. They maintain this air; whilst the few remaining sent word they ain't cotton that repellent mode of policy. And lead in mind, their polling card will be nugatory in this tiring struggle of changeover. We staring 'em carping 'bout governments, according 'em a govt should be hither wiping worries off at their side. But not for carrying out apparitions, one thing is sure; they will be all inefficient to build your dreams. Cuz times became critical, and several countries became trust territories, and are living on bailout plans.

And those that patronized those countries have begun to bend double in this plight. Political schemer ain't efficient to confront the challenge, but often obliged to fib to become the Chief Executive. Kinda call of duty turns in negative emotion, cuz constant slurs all over the place, when you come close the disgusted citizens.

Something goes wrong, they already smell a rat, when the civic responsibility not yet commenced. Where are the taken commitments? Efficiently manipulated, the no mindful persons become poverty stricken, believing on fantasies as the child. Look how they did them wrong in each hustings. They only put their whole life on applicants, who been here spit on us his fairy-tale. Behind these welters of words are obscured perfidious plans.

We are eyeing 'em decree draft bills in aid of their clan. Measures hit everywhere and became enforced laws, when it's 'bout cash issues. Peeps have tense words 'bout early warning radars that are effectuated beside beltway. According piqued folks it's a moneybox for their state, according some states it's a means to contend versus road evildoer. You can see kinda issue irritate some peeps, till some persons began to banjax kinda machines. Cuz they qualified it sickening, plus infringements are very expensive and abusive.

Deeds qualified as felon's acts by the involved states, and stated to them a tough repression, when they got 'em red-handed. Kinda peeps unveil their discrepant, spleen by a terrible frenzy. You can see some peeps made a flawless reliance toward some individuals in the first talks. Look em what they have gotten in return, these ones became thankless wretch. And yet when these ones had needed help, they entreated them as a poor devil. Here is most of human demeanor, the sex does not matter. When kinda betrayals hit feeble minded, often they ain't finding the accurate words, to qualify this treacherous attitude.

Some amongst them think to get stillness, in including some persons as responsible 'bout that let-down. They rubbed up the wrong way and became free-spoken. Learning ability suffused of scorn; even they assume the pernicious air, but they misbehave. Kinda illogical motive thrusts hostile peeps to turn in yahoo. Often the justice of people turns in iniquity, when they impotent to weather a prob, anybody close to them can be jeopardized.

We perceived the sound of fairness in numerous countries, fraternity and liberty. The one who hears 'bout all of this, will get positive thought 'bout free speech. Often nothing 'bout that is bonafide, the reality is another thing, when foreign medias are coming, all ill therapies are stashed for not engender commotions. They vaunt showing the fake scenery to some idiots, who believe everything. All of that are done for having sake from righteous homologous and to avoid attacks from global organizations which fight against discriminations, and the no respect of human's rights.

The president gets richer in kinda country whilst the population is impoverishing every day. Most of these countries become merciless, when you denounce kinda discrimination, you're condemned to exile in hiding, or you will pay the price of your offence. When these contestations are intended toward the president, often some persons amongst his entourage take some initiatives to turn your life infernal. The initiative is to mete you terrible lines, kinda negative procedure are deeply ingrained in their coercive conception.

They become fierce, before you give them hard nut to crack. There are some leaders, who are ready toss demonstrators in calaboose, till tortured them, just for they shut up their talkative mouths for they dare any-more challenging their authority. To be a weak person is synonym of an infernal life, cuz the stronger rule the roost. Across some countries you can see citizens go off at the deep end, when foreign medias stand at their side, opening to view their aversion.

By the same step trying to evidence to other countries, where freedom is topical to look how they are bossing around, whilst the govt is playing the self-righteous in front of newspersons. Kinda repression is different of some countries, where despotism is topical and exerted like a ton bricks. That obdurate repression staves them off to dare the govt, has the more reason to demo their hyper in front of foreigner's cameras. The one who steps to the fore will carry the can on the spot, when journalists pack their bags. So the govt stays clear with babblers who mumble to the correspondents.

On account this caveat nobody venture to cut across the initiated guidelines, cuz they have hectors above them. Far from handsome, those taskmasters silence citizens and infract human rights. During UN is playing diplomacy, the bloodsheds drive sensible spirits into obfuscation. A method to proceed which is tied with anarchy era; we are no more in a diplomacy world. UN is no longer respected by people and all their guideposts are not match for this shogunate.

UN is behaving as they fear to take responsibilities towards these bloodbaths. UN is proceeding as if they were abettors about these bloody massacres. The most funny is what are the role and the importance of UN in this world? If the UN is not able to face vet's holders or to try these inglorious persons; what is their importance?

This may sound funny but some countries that hold the veto shield countries where they have a self-concern. Does this strike you as being unfair? Each day they are broadcasted in the tube, talking 'bout resolution.

A turbulent world where leaders talk terms with power-mad person, and yet a highwayman is jugged swiftly when he offended. A bloody destiny, children born into those dirties and unfair warfares. Gazing at their father's or mother's eyes appalled, when fighter jets or tanks are strafing the resistance areas. Who are or who are not the resistance fighters? No one knows but they prefer to proceed to a blitzkrieg by expedience, whilst resistance fighters took the warpath, defying 'em wit' an attrition war.

Without ambiguity, UN is differing group of countries included with veto holders. Just if one of 'em disallow to lead an action through the world all the system is jammed. That odd system proven to us, that UN organization is just a masquerade. Cuz some veto's holders opt out just to preserve their interests that to lead an action in the friend country, following file. The rock oil and wampum are messing the world up, letting no chance to humanism and virtues. Everywhere in wide world scuffles are declared, an only incentive, the one to put eyes on devil's stuff.

The Tempter's message was clear, the one who detains these 2, will boss people around. From war to war tied with an only incentive (the interest). See them put forward that some countries are threats for the world integrity. What talk about them who averred no cogent evidences, proclaiming warfare then deeply looted the targeted countries? Most of wars have been initiated where big factories and oilfields are topical.

These same leaders know the virtues, and don't forget to evidence the know how in the goggle box, behind that demo they get into deep the drudges. The war for wealthiness, we ain't gonna specifying the country, neither the war. But we could hear to the receiving set that a minister who has been beaming when the swayer of a country been shot down. This man dares to declare that he hopes that his country will have several parts of markets, and most business deal. He was complacent then long for that procedures move of kind. This drongo man can only engenders contempt from wise peeps, cuz he has none wisdom.

Kinda satisfaction is suitable for greedy people, whilst several souls left toward the Day of Atonement. They are making their business in not having dead bodies travelled in the conscience. The masters of the world, only them decide who gonna survive or who gonna die in that torment. Terrifying wars initiated by these new masters of world, wars described as apocalypse. Carbonized vehicles, calcined corpses mingled with bruised areas. Kinda strain turns in guerrilla and suicide bombing.

While the regime is torturing the captured adversaries, you can see people blunder about. They are trying to flee the conflict zones toward neighboring countries. Kinda peeps were about to build their future, but propelled in refugee status. Pittances are spreading, put disgust in the spirits and occasioned the no alternative in most of minds. Rough and uncertain destiny, they are eloping from their native countries, for this so called Eldorado. During the so called Eldorado inhabitants are seeking fiercely the better days.

No matter to try your luck, but in leading in mind one place for 1million of persons. So you have seen what look like this Eldorado, if you are not a jammy you will be up your ears in debt. Nobody can be a lucky bastard to get out in being intact in this train of emotional stress, cuz life does not favor to anybody. Misery became a yucky blast of wind notified as continuum, that none senses is trained to foresee its course and his figure. Citizens are shouting out they are graduated, and they wanna a job matching with their professional skill. Is today kinda whimsy is affordable for everyone? Kinda people don't feel life doesn't move of kind nowadays. The acquired diploma can't give you, the job you pictured in your fantasies.

Have a good job is not hocus-pocus, but just based on chance nowadays. Countless people are diploma holders, but this does not prevent they keep-on to galley. Or to make as job, a job from A to Z opposed of their initial trade. The great knowledge is to cotton-on the nowadays system. Don't be astounded for those who born inside this anxiety.

They struggle against kinda concerns tied with em since the first breath. Some governments hearten their citizens to have a trade, and then to get out from daily difficulties. During unemployment is waxing, during certified people go company from company, in vain. When job centers are overcrowded, where meet dismissed people and long term non-workers. Broken hearted, several folks assured to have a trade is the same kind of trifle away. Cuz never your acquired will be appreciated.

Youthfulness see powerless an auspicious future collapses. When we rap 'bout kinda topic, we often see when a callow bloke is daunted. He becomes wide-open, and can overbalance through ill-fated side. Madden people assured that mean minded will do misdeed, to avert thy course of action. They only let to them mc-job; even their skills provide other abilities. Expected you will come across the honcho, who can give you the way out. We often denote among manures, we can run across kind hearted. They are pointing rogue districts qualified as traffickers' mansion.

What is their responsibility 'bout this crisis of decency? Is that they tempted to wrack this prob correctly? Or are they rubbed the wrong way to end it? Questions are travelling in some minds. Why they wanna be rogue? Is the result of long term of galley? Is that they will take that route, if they were in positive stance? Is that leaders are cognizant that their manner to govern present several blackout? Only God knows, but a thing is sure from doubt, only the initiated system determines 80 percent of a country functioning.

Deprivation ain't an excuse to step into breach of law or acting as yobbo. Destitution and suffering are tense struggles, where numerous persons gotta get out with genuine stamina; even there are concerns all over the world. Instead of gonna get the struggle with a getter's mind. Some people are spending time to yammer, comprehensible attitude, but ain't suitable in a plight. Everything goes fast the dream until the collapse. Seeing their wishes don't work, many people step in mortgage line, taking loan to achieve some fantasies.

Thinking this can give them a little lull in their daily prob. For several moods here's a scheme to get relieve in that financing deficit. Opposite people's thought, it's o'er there, where troubles arose. Some people don't comply with that procedure (the loan). Cuz many people get out from that negative system, initiated by sharks, more hapless and desponded. None furtherance, kinda troubles incited mindful peeps to ponder twice, before to sink into that dirt financial collapse.

Temptations of life drove several persons towards beyond repair, when they face financial sharks. A negative reality when you are debt ridden; another hardship when your mind urges you to make step backwards. Is that people can make ends meet without loan in this financial crisis? It has been said that God fearing men, misery can't mess them up till they commit the wrongness. According them kinda ordeal is linked with traced out destiny then the best remains to come. Kinda philosophy is so far from nowadays mental-makeup.

If that sentence is certified, we can assure this mood rarefied. Each coming day, poverty and life's temptations are making victims. A person who alleged to believe a prayer, plus believes the authenticity of God, must practice as his religion asked. Therefore he will be always a follower of second zone like most of us. A value judgment based on human criticism, at the side of God the theory can be opposed. Nowadays there are lots of followers of second zone. By this manner this world is moving, followers of second zone became greatest luxury. Cuz nowadays it became so hard, for numerous people to think a while 'bout God.

Because they are deeply trapped into worldly, consigned to oblivion that the Old-Nick is behind that fake scenery. They are disappointed, when they light upon the genuine reality behind that fake landscape. Is life worthwhile to forget God? This question is valid for some persons who believe 'bout his existence, and his flawless mercifulness. In those critical times, some people think that the immigration drove myriad predicaments in their countries.

According some drongo citizens, the immigration does not juicy for them. So tell us how much the price of resident card is every year. Aliens became invaders ya ears can hear in dirty mouths. Most of em talk the system attracts these ones, what kinda system you are talking about? The same system you are talking about turned you greedy and idiot. It's why you have the time scrutinize in it and be on the look out as bulldogs.

Liable persons can aver in some countries, strangers are not respected, cuz they are deemed as invaders. You can see nowadays, when hustings are topical, some candidates wanna egg immigration on, or get oath to regulate illegal immigrants. For those people get rights to move freely, as all citizens. Often kinda lead is done by a few politicians. Not hard to get it banned according antagonists. Bogus it's beyond their ken, prevent kinda move became complex. Stowaways will be enticed and will surge from everywhere in the globe. Candidates of antagonists mouthed they have fed up 'bout the immigration and aliens.

They don't waver, when they state baleful talks, cuz the perniciousness is as saliva in komodo's mouth. I am doubled up 'bout that mood, the most idiot will cry with his heart out tomorrow. 'Bout political, the applicants aim to entice voters. People, who put system failure on immigrants, are born in founding immigration's process in motion. The immigration machine is very circuitous, never discourses will impede it. Immigration is tied with stakes and accounts. Immigration was favored, and forwarded by most of governments. Cuz they had need hands to raise myriad projects. Immigration became a custom that exceeds several governments.

To become elected some applicants aim to shape a cause 'bout some governments failures, just to confuse the issue and to get the simples muddled. You will have a good cry tomorrow, cuz they are tricksters. You will be queasy, when you will see all that detestation and the insecurity they generated, of course if you have been duped by their smooth talks. No doubt if you are accomplice with these schmucks, cuz your dark desires will be fulfilled.

The evil spirit is the no interesting dirt; turned you as blockhead then propelled the rest of you in the nothingness. Birds of a feather flock together. You can hear in desperate mouths that the immigration brought hoodlums. Peep at everywhere (outskirts, greatest towns, council states; you will figure out that malicious mischief proceeds everyplace, fed by poverty and discrimination. The first demon is the one who exploits the people's idiocy. The factor that drove malicious mischief at the height of its power is very plain. Your so called mental makeup can't plan it out; the world is what it is, for donkey's years.

To state kinda idiocy is the thinking of a clot; anyway what goes around comes around. The beau-monde shaped a clan while another clan sees the light, and became hard that these 2 cohabitate together. Some people have their fill of aggro as most of people flipping out of kind. Each passing day, I saw numerous people buoy-up assaultive behavior; a vehemence that unveils some folks, when they are out of savvy.

If you try to ferret out, you will descry people, who felt hurt by the state of mind of catty people. Brutality can rule a time but not all time. They are disgruntled by the public's opinion; and often have a blatant behavior. All I known, we ain't run on the same wavelength, cuz the fall guy our clan brushes him aside any days. A little strife, then you will spend time in police custody, whatever contentious. Most of people became jumpy and attracted by the strife, if you are clever, you will stay aside from that shit. Everyplace you go become same. To face money dearth, folks are ready for some practices.

Poverty brought foxiness, obliging some people to have a practical turn of mind, otherwise they will not see out. And that constancy drove most of them toward gambling den. A place; where you can pick up dough swiftly and in losing it hurriedly, if you don't curb your ardent want. Bingo hall always suffused by stake, sprain and despair, and a thrill to be conned. To say that some have-nots are obliged to fast, cuz they can't afford don't engender positive poignancy, but an odd lip service. They allege to be regarded 'bout the topic, sly persons you're.

Myriad rapines wind the world; several persons decry it, whilst numerous people no longer respect their fellow citizen. Lack of parental education or forgetful persons, we noticed that this frame of mind is intricate. God proves to us, we all are sinners; God does not need to do gesture, but let us with our nous to appreciate the good and evil. Just for those who are quick witted, but not the narrow minded. They fear to utter 'bout religions, most of people turn a blind eye, when you begin to be disturbing most of people flee you.

When you assure you're devoted 'bout your religion, people ain't convinced 'bout it, cuz leading in mind that the devotion is no longer topical. World events drove people's mind in mental disturbance, until they ease up to Old Nick. Just your faith towards God can save you in that challenge that you can't get out intact in being faithless. Instead of to cope, they go off the rails (how to be in good faith, in such world; the desolation became spooky each day passing).

A question to avoid if you don't wanna being interned loony bin, God is the master and can make a halt to damaging things. If God does not intervene 'bout world's events, he has his reasons. Sizeable do not sink in delirium, continue to be God-fearing men. Don't monkey around trying to make out what going on, just look the decline's signs and go to decrypt their meanings in a genuine definition. It seems that anyone has own his reasons that defines his demeanor.

They throw you a challenge when you're at the side of 'em (some people look dagger at you). They are full of themselves, as they don't have the call of natures. As we mouthed before do not pay heed 'bout these kinda soft touch (not trying to make out what going on) it takes all sorts to make a world. Most of us favor coitus prior feelings, cuz they got worrying mania in parts of nookie as neurotic. 'Bout that bed of roses they have myriad parts. Wise people are seeing that the duplicity is spreading in the world. That dirt became fixation for sex maniac, men or women the sex does not matter in this sinning era.

World is changing face at all levels, whilst a state of mind encourages the probity, whereas mores are degraded. The consumer society drove people to be without compunction. If today most of world citizens became lured by side issue, is their fault? I don't dare to mouth who is the one who is not trapped in the glut, cuz I know there is a few remaining who have no time 'bout that superfluity, or who have not the means. Some men apprised if a fella got an achievement; the success is often built by his wife. And if this one bites the dust, this disillusionment is often created by his wife.

Are you assenting with this issue, in knowing most of people drove themselves in failures? Anyway if you don't come to a conclusion 'bout your fate, your fate will decides for you. And this is not in this dark era that the manner to live would launchs toward positive trend. They haven't compunction to quench their wants in this worldly. You can eye them offer their offspring to most bidders, whilst these maniacs are dribbling by what they are seeing. 2 sides are thinking it's the solution, but the beginning of the biggest lost.

Bad deeds that some cowards practicing, they will gonna vindicate it front of God; nobody will bolt for kinda moments. You can observe many people wear religious signs without figure-out their genuine meaning. Easy to spell God's name, but follow his guidances became uphill for numerous souls. Just to see people's behavior and you will twig the gist of that sentence. Without stamina, frustration, angst, mental suffering will be your infernal routine.

Ugly face of worldly, bread is unavoidable, then making rules; got it allows you to hobnob everybody. You ain't got it, you're pointed as vulgar beggar, even they don't tell you. Upper crust thinks that the have-nots embody the troubles of society. Every clan defines the other as waif. But we can notify a huge part of the citizenry is shitty by their deeds and nobody can expect something positive from em. All these dissents whilst another category of citizens bow out to fight the just cause.

Some people are trying to acquaint the petite bourgeoisie; doubtless they are the suitable prey of scammers), a scheme for these sons-of-guns to rip-off a bit of their total assets. When most of 'em commiserate you, lead in mind they have a yield through this bond. Any times they carp-about but when comes time to assert themselves, most of 'em disappear (the talkative). The outliving became overriding than pride, cuz human's qualities are lost and are given the right of way to shortcomings. You will see them striving to resemble to headliners or men of means.

Trivial for some folks and whacko for others, but if they often ken how most of these people were down in the dumps earlier to be men of means, they going to ponder twice time. Often noticed when someone got an achievement, often his early history was tough. Deeds of some peeps ain't heartfelt, why only whammy can muster them, when most of time they could take a part in drudges' torments. 'Bout brainwave God is strongest, a conjecture objurgated by some folks and hosted by others.

The world is polluted by mendacious and cruel peeps. Where enlighten the truth is perceived as serious lapse according the filthy file, where the verity bothers some unfair or criminal minds. You gotta veil your face before to face reprisals. Anyway some people don't care about, argued the truth must be unveiled despite some consequences, if mandatory. Through the quest of understanding God throws a little signal about his absolute ingenuity.

A sent signal for the clever minds, how you can plan out to be in front of a person in being unable to reason out his native language. And can have another morphology than you, God likes the diversity, and sent you the message, peeps don't. We are obliged in a sense to love everything that emanates from his ingenuity. Therefore the fail is guaranteed. Some people boasting, then behaving as if they can step through everything their fantasy pointed. You are behaving of kind and God-fearing men are laughing, cuz you are underneath from understanding. You will puzzle out the day you will scnesce, cuz you took this amiss.

A childish behavior that never leaves you in peace, and gives the right of way to the prime of life. Sometimes you can meet a black sheep, don't challenge him through that line, cuz you will meet the society's sentence, even you were offended. If you step so far you will toast God's sentence. What will be God's judgment in knowing that new society is Old-Nick game field, again another question in abeyance? People bill and coo in world streets. They appear every with a so called sincere love. But they embody the overwhelming rate of divorce, if you mind to them.

We are seeing that anytime, during some marriages you can eye the wastage. Event gathering plaudits, lip service and the envious minds, a pleasant or hypocrite atmosphere that veils dustup, ups and downs and a bit felicity, once the cohabitation becomes topical. Who are these world citizens who make loan or who use savings to achieve the marriage, splurging money then can't keep the marriage virtues so long.

Some peeps go apeshit, when we stick the "wastage word" through the sentence. We don't care cuz the realistic minds already make out that this behavior is crude according world situation. Several weasel situations then couples face split up. How many persons facing inserity in the couple, cuz the wife or the husband does not respect the virtues of marriage and engagements?

We eyewitness broken marriages either by lack of positive attitude or by lack of confidence, or to have fed up seeing same spouse. To live the end of a love engenders terrible hardships if the love was sincere. Few people arrive to keep head up in accepting what happening to them. The thing turns in bitter lane to cross, if the love was sincere for one between them, but alleviation for the one who had fed up 'bout the relation. Most of no sincere peeps don't losing time and become infatuated with another man or woman during the split up. The path of reconstruction is so bitter for the sincere person, cuz he will meet the solitude, the depression then the convalescence if he has a genuine stamina.

During or out from troubles kinda persons will be animated by vindictiveness to the opposed sex. Most of people have afraid when it about marriage, a fear that brought a new trend the one, do not privilege the marriage. Kinda tendency drove most of people to favor the amusement instead of get engagement, as if they were adept of misogamy. It seems that most of us will encounter the divorce procedure in the course of their life; a kinda verity that some people began to accept according negative trend they are seeing. Kinda negative gives fear and no mind chill out. Most of us run the risk to lose everything someday, either by the run-ins, duplicity, routine, opacity or lack of integrity.

Everyone strives to overawe the spouse, but often loses guts if one of them shows himself hard-bitten. Not easy to live satisfyingly with his spouse during years. Those who have the suitable wife can't boast, someday this ease can turn up in nightmare if that one is a thespian. If the wife demeanor is reliable, this achievement does not emerge from the husband skills. Without doubt they have been present at by God in that success.

No one is up to sensing the harmful thing that will annihilate his cleverness in the long run. Even to take all time to know him or to know her, never you will be sure that you made the suitable choice. The one, who will hurts you, often knows or does not know that he will be your tormenter later, then throwing you in the chasm. The world is rotted by wampum and salacious minds, dirty business better to look that shit then stand away from it, if you ain't wanna be one of their victims.

Questioned a friend, saying him if someone calls you "infidel, what are you going to answer him. He replied to me this going to make him giggle, what so fun bro, I said him. He responded, cuz more than half between us are infidels nowadays. And got inkling that the infidelity does not disturb most of people, or mentalities became shameless. To come across ladies 'man or loose women became run of the mill, gotta consider your husband or your wife as comrade. But not your best confidant, cuz never you will soothsay the future. Kinda tension incites some peeps do not divulge secrets that they must not disclose in the spouse's ears.

This remains the one way, for not being surprised in this negative world. The half about you is sufficient. Just what you wanna the spouse to know is enough, and like that you can be still. If you already reveal all 'bout you, you can have regrets, only a dependable wife or a trustworthy husband deserves it. A reluctance if the spouse is a manipulator, hope never you gonna terminate your love affair. Because if this woe comes to happen, this can be an object of avenge or blackmail, if you slated some boo-boo you have done. It not always kinda ruptures terminate amicably as we said.

We got misgivings 'bout that. We are in this fear that motivated our reticence. Development brought some intricacies nowadays. The development can be an iniquity, and maybe be an unnerving weapon. The constant use of development into unfair situation torn the world apart then created an immeasurable disaster. The auto destruction will remains on surface as long as peeps don't go to the positive.

The foul-up inside peeps' mind is recurrent; it seems that third world countries are no longer the only spot where journalists go to prove poverty cases. The illness, debts, crisis, crimes and misery in all its bearings behind everybody's doors. You can be made of money this stance can't hide your eyes to see that stinky misery. You can be made of money this stance will spares you to have luxury need. You can be made of money this stance will not prevent you to have call of natures as others.

Of course you are shivered about what poverty does around, cuz you have fellow feeling. Only an evil minded can be insensitive about that constant shit. You have compunction or not, stare what misery does to you, altered your habits as we were in a plague. They are living in gated community, being always accompanied by bodyguards by fear to get misery's effects. Anybody is under poverty pressure when he looks his manner to live. To bonk in being teenager or of age, smoke and drink then became blotto is a fashion in nowadays world. When a fella and a bird should have sex, they were think 'bout it twice time.

The virginity was the honor, but eros and interests are taken advantage. Peeps had shame when they fornicate, had the shame to meet themselves. But nowadays make love is linked with performance, and the girl doesn't hesitate to rate you after the intercourse. Kinda respect that the human being had kept is deleted. Most of them shoot a film 'bout their sexual intercourse, naked their body everywhere then to sell it on the net. Without shame the body of so many people became goods the sex does not matter.

Some people drink alcohol and smoke because the neighbor smokes or drinks. They ape what others are doing, just to be fashionable. The sex is everywhere in the streets, on telly and deeply incrusted in people's mind. All that tied with a peculiar perversity and turn up in reciprocal salacity. Most of guys can't look a woman without think achieving a hard carnal knowledge. What about wenches? Anyway they have nymphomaniacs at their side.

Through this disarray there are famous persons, either men or women, but nobody can get them red handed. Some people live through this trauma. The ploy artists haven't face, and they amble beside people as trustworthy citizens. But they become predators when the occasion arises. After the drug, the sex became the means the most profitable to earn money. But we already know the sex isn't free of charge, cuz that's an industry. Often when it is gratis you are beside a nymphomaniac.

Otherwise you gotta pay the price, before to achieve the sexual congress. Sometimes this transaction is so far to be dirt-cheap, but this not afraid people till incited some between 'em to expense their pays in kinda transactions. No scarce to meet already married men or these legendary flighty women driving to perform the peculiar businesses far from curious looks. Through a shameless ambiance, without care the spouses are waiting at home as silly being. The vandalism, the high society caricatured young citizens into the world, involved or not implicated in that culture crisis.

They have no time 'bout the discernment for others, but they directly spared the children of famous citizens. No doubt they will be the son or the daughter of anybody, cuz they are bourgeois. What to say 'bout caricatured young citizens, only when the first trouble arises the anti-young citizens get smile. Department stores became fortress, and equipped with that new tech in every nook. Some clerks beside their managers look them as thug when they step in. Ordaining to the security agent to follow them, as they hunt 'em down. If this sturdily guy haven' tact or have no intelligence, he will throw his weight around, till the tension arises inside every mind.

The inevitable scuffle is here and the legendary cops who seemed to get bored become active. Proud 'bout that task, cuz they have the occasion to perform their little authority. Sometimes reactions are normal created by frustration or the lack of respect. Underlining a stealer hasn't age, and an accurate appearance; a daily discrimination toward some people who seem to be penniless.

They are focusing on them, whilst the so called attractive person is giving them the fake move. Sometimes you can see young peeps discussing in housing estate then cops commence to intensify the patrols. Stare fiercely and trying to make out the goal of that gathering, they throw the first hostilities. The relations are tense; the decency should be always topical in every mind, even dissents. An odd obsession confuses their minds thinking all young citizens are no law abiding citizens.

In the meantime young citizens are also glad 'bout that bringing-about, cuz they also have the opportunity to launch an intifada. That situation became abstruse; hoodlums among young citizens nobody can negate it. Several people stated that the police beat some young people in hiding. Constables allege these young citizens are real blackguards. Gunfights, turf wars, drug traffic the police stations are under pressure and some families try do not see that their progeny became injurious for the society.

Nothing disturb some parents, just to get stuff from their children attract them. The comings and goings of their children in police custody or in sin bin disturb them anymore from the moment their children relieve them on financial expenses. The worldly is especially here to teach to blind people a hard and bitter lesson later. To follow this fake system will engenders your imminent lost; only you will come near of the realistic persons to water till create a pity. The mindful will tells look what he made of his life. We often noted numerous catastrophes wind the world with countless human losses.

It became unavoidable that every year some awful occurrences blow drastically the world. Kinda events terrify some people, whereas others like these terrible occurrences. When kinda woe appears somewhere, it torn the involved country apart then alters it in topsy-turvy. Only a tragedy can gathered people for various reasons. Myriad cataclysms turn in trafficking, when there are people victim of casualty.

Especially in developing countries, some so called benefactors or benefactresses rush to sojourn in kinda countries to make inhuman transactions. The most widespread is the organ trafficking, a booming trafficking that engenders huge amounts of money for traffickers. This human exploitation is doing before the eyes of persons deeply gnawed by the want. They have no alternative, when we decrypt their manner to live, cuz they are dead broke. They are ready to transact, when traffickers solicit them.

They don't care if they profit about human misery, only their self-concern takes advantage on their common sense. Even there are some convicted traffickers 'bout that human trafficking. This system of rules to provoke dissuasion seems do not be dissuasive in their mind, cuz this does not dampen their way of looking at things. After suicide cases inquiry, we make out why often some people have suicidal drive. Our investigation gave us four motives that led some people towards beyond repair. This situation explained by itself.

Often after been a man of means, numerous people lose their megabucks. And in front of this plight, they haven't guts, and required stamina to keep their head up then to deal with it. Twice motive concern persons who always have hard life, and who seem to live in an endless dark tunnel, where quandaries arise anytime. They have taken this close because things go wrong, when they always try to initiate. Third decision is motivated by a human loss, we often see people blow a gasket, because their spouse abandon 'em or a close parents died.

And the last motive concern people who solicit euthanasia as regarding hard suffering they endure. That God helps them to find the peace. Are these motives worthwhile to achieve a suicide? Except people who solicited euthanasia, because only God knows their suffering, only God can judge them. The suicide is defined as unholy, only we can tell that. But everyone gotta turn it aside. Numerous people did that, without aim to know, if this suicide goes to hurt their relatives or close friends.

The plight led dangerously numerous chicks to make baby opportunistically, to have allowances afterward. How many they are to make baby without sincere love? To make baby became lucrative for numerous flighty women, a profitable occasion, allowances, alimonies pointed as inciter. In some areas the talkative person are undesirable, cuz the noise can harm to. Even this mouth assures a verity, antagonists ready to argue him down. Lies are custom, world is weaved of lies, tied with lots of interests. Some peeps can kill your close parents, and they mourn with animated heart of dark desires.

Till hypocrisy hits the place the mourning day. Not knowing often some instigators pass to present condolences. They appreciate and remember everyday about that act, don't waver hypocrisy lies behind. The devil's child was beside them with a trustworthy appearance, but ready to reiterate, when someone will antagonizes his stinky plans. The humanism is only suitable for feeble minded according some talks.

The lack of humanism is only venerated by devil's children, till the day he will confutes his intentions to them. At the same jiffy, he will define them as unaware. A dark glance will emerge from his legendary red eyes, whilst your eyes run tears; cuz realized you will adjoin him in hell's chambers. Every wrong man must attend, no possible U-turn when launched in that gangway of all torments. Again take heed 'bout that statement far from balderdash. Worldly sank them, of course partygoer they chosen, take no heed or forgetting the gist of revelations.

Futilities already took advantage, but in the first gale sent by God another history is 'bout to get started Qualified as the end of time by thinkers. Dirty time that futilities of stinky worldly will abruptly consigned to oblivion by common run people. Your cup of wine, nightclubs, and blunt left you in the lurch as vulgar being who will return dust. Your arrogance and haughty air been suddenly brushed out by this ever seen genuine shiver.

Trying to escape but that's another history, cuz crack of doom in sight. God's kingdom is coming with ever hear noise. These devils' children beg mercy. Only the devil abandons his acolytes, when he fatally led them astray. Innocents and acolytes with terrible heartbeats. Anybody will be appalled, when they leak all their history word by word. Well-kept histories before the world torn apart by divine will. they preferred to render account the day of reckoning, but the day turned topical.

Even they only perceived misery on television the reality became topical everywhere. The plight incited them to realize the gap between 3 universes, most of 'em been stormed by the wind misery. Taking a bash in the conscience, then the awareness arose in 'em to see the true face of this changing world and its dark functioning system. The universe of moneyed people, the universe of go-getter, and the universe of excluded people from worldly. A life to live and hard to be positive, some frustrated persons sustaining.

But their misconceptions blew wide open before anybody's eyes, seeing the way that kinda occurrences can be harmful. The brainy persons became argus-eyed do not iterate identical missteps, figured out his own integrity and character can be tested. Some people have no moral support and become talkative, when they face a dainty prob. Trying to get a relief, the only goal of their act, they confessed, when the so called friends dissipate it in anybody 's ears, after carefully hear all the sad history. They were beside them, as if their goal was to divulge the moral suasion of that feeble minded.

The financial crisis isn't a little depression and does not only engender a little ado, but hazardous pothers. Breakages, endless panel discussions and guerrillas between constables and rioters definite the chafe in each spirit. Countries become pauperized and tied with negative waves. Whilst the ambiance shaping a kinda gloominess, unremitting solicitude and tensions of all kinds. The dark chapter of our era, we can't produce a denial, 'bout this changing world, austerity plans in every mouth and in every spirit provoking a fit of hysterics.

We haven' choosing, they have the dangerous habit to handle the situation and to decide on future, and seem that they are the only persons who are capable to checker 'bout that slump. All that after several years of mistakes. Politicians, most of 'em came from of bon ton, do they really are the persons of that endless and stinky plight? Do they really make out the real definition of need? A depression that propels some countries to bailout plans in bailout plans, austerity plans tied with a terrible economic recession, whilst other countries are waiting to sink into this infernal circle as we early said.

They were law abiding citizens till the day that the babylone's effects altered them in bloodthirsty spirit. This new society is the cause of this dark barbarity, only its suitable name is babylone according each day occurrences. To have a positive attitude became a challenge tied with a sure-fire force of will, cuz no positive wave is detectable. The world is bisected, the clan of idiots and those of cognizant minds.

Each mind will reconnoitre his place according his manner to live and his everyday acts. You can eye inevitable clash between state of minds, each of 'em is persuaded to hold the veracity and the best standpoint on the other. No need to have a huge conversance to make out the wrong insight. I fear for the following generation. I fear for em, if they refer to this hopeless society. The society has a recondite face which has not yet emerged.

Hope help nowhere, cuz they blinded too I am not wondering what will be my future life, but just my tomorrow life, cuz each day is a tiring challenge to succeed and face the devil. Shaped sentence for cognizing minds, to warn em that their lives will be tied with a constant consternation. How they can hope that the bloodshed and let-downs be annihilate, if their own mental-makeup isn't positive? Some countries are incontestably powerful before anybody's eyes, till most of them consigned to oblivion the source of that ephemeral strength. This undisputable power is only effective in common run of people, a mental labor that should be blatant.

But these countries become muted in the first hit, when a vis major comes into sight then hits the area. In the troubles they temporarily lost their concert, but always want to keep their self-appearance into such disaster. Even disaster unites some persons, laughs-at are welcomed in the hostiles areas. An attitude to condemn the regime they consider supercilious and enemy. Anyway the only thing I retain about these tensions is the strength of God; he only sends a little hardship for that a country or the world sinks into turmoil, whilst its citizens bow down with terrible cries of pain. .

Some of us don't see that they must step backwards according every day lessons. They are so blind till they embody the 666's landscape. Some peeps became enemies or treated those who try ratiocinating em as archaic minds. Those you sell short have more chance to put a small change in your palm's hands in coming years. These same will be yer rescuers in some infernal situations. If you reminisce 'bout advices they tempted to infuse you, when you were trapped in the den of blinds' clan.

You must manifest a genuine regard according the pertinence of their mental-makeup. They gone through the obvious reality, early handed by another argus eyed. Evidence that did not spurt into your mind in the first talk. Worldly sucked your sanity. Unbearable situation everywhere, cuz the conjuncture stinks. If you haven't the pertinence of each coming situation, you will sink; we constantly live on quick sand. Instead of have an enlightening glance toward the words, they have chosen to turn a blind eye to their authentic illustration. Most of people had the mind focused in criticism, when they were throwing sentence in their vision.

They don't care and misbehave, when occasion arises. Their vision was not large as their spirits did not have the capacity achieving the positive perspectives. Some people and leaders crying all over the place crisis, till the eye-drums burst from that negative sound. Of course they all allege to know how rub it out, or how to face these stinky situations.

But most of 'em must not forget they also are the first cause of that plight that seems irreversible. Is that their statements are really genuine, or they pretending? Their greediness led us here; a fact is sure from doubt, if people stop stealing to advantage the accounts of their countries. These ones will recover their financial balance step by step. They also talking about insecurity that emerging in other countries, but deeply concealed the dirt that booming, guns, illicit things took control in their respective countries.

You can't rub what you are talking about, cuz this really exceeds you in at all levels. We all need to pray do not come across the devil's son will give us the fatal meet. Devil got strong and stronger each coming day, cuz he grows by our dire deeds. Mister Satan everything is reachable for you here, and then asked where God fearing men are? Got retort from one of these imps, several traitors all over the world nowadays, then added rare is to meet God's disciple in these iterative troubles, where most of 'em left their identity behind.

Already made out that they don't need to have a hunting area, the Tempter's army is achieving easily. Brothels are localized as block of flats in a quarter, a triviality to have a catch sight of kinda places. They don't pay attention bout God's words, and they blunted by this system, but look how they became, vulgar attitude, they proud of it as poor bugger. Worst, most of em don't make out they already are brats. Some countries already decriminalized some questionable activities that lead straight towards the libertinage. Instead of try to bar kinda comportment, they cede where they must struggle against.

Only 'em can demystify it, even some talks launch toward a history of money recovering. It seems that Satan has anymore need to apply a pull on people, cuz it seems a few persons remain to be faithful to the all mighty, more than the half already trapped in svengali's den. God's followers only need to kneel down imploring him to shake this disease out. But don't forget, when God is really angry the retribution will have another effect that you can't define.

Our clan really prefers his silence than his punishment; already know his judgment will intercede sooner than later. I don't wonder why God doesn't intervene concerning the arrogance of peeps. Cuz already know a goon who will not escape from his trackers does not worth to spend time. God does not have the time to teach people how to cohabitate since he gave them the fundamentals basis to live as humans but not as beasts. I really giggle at when they 'bout to gazette figures concerning the decrease of the aggro. Ridiculous if the society is so clean and no fierce, why you fear to amble in all corners.

All that insecurity will be always topical, if discrimination is turned in civilization. You spat fable, won't get it cuz no suitable to prudent persons. No need to have brainwashed from fickle minded we anyway game for stability, a positive enterprise. We often try to out from the trivial, a way to prove we are genius, but in vain. So called genius misled as donkey for years and unable leading himself in the right conception.

X-rated areas or sites, they try to struggle against the scourge, shouting in everybody's ears "if you're not grownup, you will not be allowed browsing inside porn sites. They are lascivious and with this lust of sex, most of children and adults mixed together use foxiness to cloak their real character. The society meets an alarming rate of rape and sexual offences achieved by different individuals. Kids know how to lead sexuality as mature adults, and also know how to romance more mature than them. Sensual delight in all its bearings became a triviality, and unveiled all secrets.

Often you can witness several minors charming adult males, and if these men aren't clear-headed they will dwell straight in slammer. Either enticement steps up and became a monomania, or they really wanna easiness through a life with constant profligacy. Anyway they will get wrong, even most of men announced do not able recognizing accurately the difference between major and minor females.

They related that birds became precocious, when others spit words on 'em "never rely on 'bout gaits, cuz nowadays people are so gifted for pretence". Everywhere you can see so many people get fresh supplies inside bins of department stores. Destitution in progress, a behavior directly tied with conjuncture. Often these scavengers haven't the pick, and several among them are wage earner. In that new quest of foods, there are those who are completely banned of the system.

What to say bout wage earners who are confronting that new manner to live? According some talks few persons engaged that endeavor to make savings. Also to attract people's attention that non outdated goods can be always used, even deadline is not largely reached. But no doubt 'bout major part that took that initiative, they have done this, cuz they daily face a hard money dearth. Today some people who take heed about that indigence wonder, if there were not some associations as "Resto du Coeur" what will be the density of this new wind of misery.

Only a good hearts and clever persons can initiate kinda structures to feed have-nots. They struggle against that ambient pauperisation which is increasing, enterprise applauded by anybody. And yet kind-hearted are not always men of means, but decide to share what God granted them. As we saw everywhere, most of caller-up have job. In the past, only bums and job seekers had needed to knock "Resto du Coeur's doors". A quest that most of 'em had difficulty to achieve, cuz they thought 'bout their dignity. But nowadays seeing several people knocking associations' doors to have foods supply.

They have any-more apprehension, cuz they realized more than the half of citizens solicits em. What tell about pretenders who are counting their infinite banknotes, free from the criticism observation? ******* Treacherous bosses shout that an unfair system is coming into sight. Can you explain us the unfair system that turned the life of have-nots infernal for years? Of course your attitude gives your clique comfort and notoriety, a way to be indispensable pieces of the system.

They got real fear 'bout incomes taxes that rub out your extra incomes. They ready to leave in the lurch several employees and they get stranded to clash with financial sharks. Bosses are trying to fly the coop from what they are pointing out as injustice, who tells you the justice is topical in the world. They resent the reform whilst some presidents strive to quash selfish attitude. You begin to understand what the minorities are braving whilst you were raving everywhere in world famous streets.

No rave-up here only come boarding to the balloon that winds gust, you will bitterly appreciate the charm. Some governments are in the quest to compel anybody to be law-abiding citizen. Even if before they had been championed from stink realities by cronies, but shade comes to them, witnessing the tax-shield poleaxes by conscious peeps as mends in relation to their egotism. We only related facts; we ain't having quizzical state of mind as our sentences may be defined. We all need being mindful, a rush state of mind can lead us in cardboard city.

The real matter is not what they enduring, but at the end how several among them will be spared do not find themselves ruined, and probably to frequent cardboard cities. It seems worst remains to come knocking doors at random, so the future is dark. Bosses and wealthy men describe it as kinda manhunt. Trough these dense quarrels, some wealthy persons resort to tax heavens to breath awhile. Some fallen presidents or members of their respective clans have faced a first bawling out, and sent to criminal court. Whilst some amongst them shout from housetops a secret plan, others confess to lighten the sentence.

Vexed citizens shout them down, cuz they make out they were the fall guy for donkey's years. The world hosts numerous men of means, crooks or trustworthy merchant banker; only the clan's members can have a glance through that muddle. But some states' coffers are empty, great evasion tied with trafficking of all kinds.

Countries are facing a chronic deficit, they can't make ends meet, whilst billions falling through the cracks, to bilk to taxes every year. Their egoism stimulates them to leave their countries to escape from troubles. Some peeps fiercely shouted they discharge themselves income taxes why not others, you can hear in every mouth. You ain't getting out from trouble, cuz peeps repine. International financial centre" you want that like insignia, thinking they ain't seeing the soft shenanigan. You abnegate that we call your organization tax-havens.

Try to actuate other men of means to join 'em, advertising "we can change the world" You wanna more tricksters, I wonder how you can have a sleep the night? This new clique cumbers the democracy. You all in the heazy, it's why they zeroed on your suspicious activity. After moneyed people, what about the rest of citizens who ante up their incomes taxes? Several among them cough up their taxes but yammer every year with the afflicted amounts. They expected a small hairdab, then abruptly made out they haven't choice and means to do a monkey business.

Several among em resort to fraud when declarations are topical, cuz they die hard. They also shout out and become frustrated hater when they come across the moneyed persons who subscribed in tax-havens. They can be in cahoots, because they also chisel to lighten their expenses. When declaration 'bout incomes taxes are topical, people don't arrive to fill their income tax form. And yet every year it's the same exercise.

We know that only money interesting them, ready to the duty, the public servants help them every year to fill the income tax return. But nevertheless the problem holds on, they even ready to behave as unskilful persons, it's very difficult to achieve that task they assured. But the others freak out, saying they get fed up to foot the tax assessment, it's why they don't take heed 'bout. It's a manner to evidence their aversion, "empty vessels make the most noise. How they can mouthed evolution, when the word contribution seems consigning to oblivion? The ambiance ain't habinar; argus-eyed peeps are conscious 'bout the eminent infelicity.

Horse-sense apprised clever minds then throws em in the know 'bout that plight which can turn in Harry Mason for several persons, if states treasures are blank. They all mouthing that crisis turned em off, but forgotten their mental make-up is a huge factor of that hot water. The double-dealing became a habitude and numerous people became gifted fraudsters. Sharp practice thrown some countries in troubles, results are hallucinating, cuz billions vaporized. They try swaying they are pure as the driven snow. Governments query kinda talks, and don't do them a solid. They consider them as truants and ain't falter arraigning the first trickster who plays smart.

Away from skeptic eyes they assured money favors the brave, don't figure out that their business can come into light someday, and even money talks. When the cat's away the mice will plays they keep on breaching as burghers, but fear them when procedures come into sight. A manner to aver their closure, whilst an interminable game of hide and go seek begins.

The revenue tariff linked with local residence tax, both turned peeps mad as a March hare by its fare. Cost living tied with this context of use jockey most of em to move toward haram initiative as last resort. We are responsible of something according our attitude. They have egomania comportment, rushed in some lands to achieve customary robbery.

It seems a little puff of majority-rule is about to get actuate to decimate all shady dealings till the palm-greasing. Peeved denizens met up crusaders that the system gets their dander up. They make debate in television studios, encouraging militants to revolt versus vampires, and those they shield to have better life on em. Fiery dictates 'em to make insurrection in large scale. They launched in debates trying to evidence that plight that they also find themselves trapped. They nourish the fighting spirit in viewers' mind; even several among em prefer perpetrating strong demonstration that is nothing than a showdown.

During kinda disturbances that incite troubles, some persons try to persuade people to achieve things with pacifism. In kinda mental strain been achieved several coups and dense uprising committed in ruthless step. Bloody combats and genocides that often led in criminal court instigators of kinda battue. Some heads of state are designate as oppressor, cuz they transformed their countries in monarchy system and in dangerous clans. They fiercely cling on power till engender the topsy-turvy Dom.

Several dirt files they hide from prying eyes that can lead em into hell on earth, if opposition party seizes kinda fishy files, troubles arise then lead citizens into dark days. Myriad exterminations for an idiotic goal; irrational incentive they handle as mainspring. Injudicious talks your ears can hear when they are in the joint. They ready to combat but they are incapable to conjecture the tomorrow's aftermaths (the new fighter). These new righter of wrongs alluded when the president is overthrown, the situation will be abruptly incontrovertible.

These new battlers of the freedom think they will integrate the govt then being assigned somewhere as executive. Malfeasances been noticed, the reign wreaks havoc all progressive strategies. New righter of wrongs engender havoc after putsch been completed. They killed each other; insurrections turn raw whilst international community noticed then remains docile. We all witness myriad carnages in camera, engendered by despots or cross-purposes. What's the efficacy of these so called righter of wrong; another question in abeyance. I don't know their virtues, how their state of mind is?

But their ways ain't intelligible, very talented making discourse and elaborates trysts that most of peeps ain't able to disclose. Inevitable masquerade the embittered eyes are seeing, kinda occurrences bother anymore, if they ain't the injured party. I have impression to view and hear same headlines on T.V and radio. Tiring subjects that seem perpetual, international community became laughable, some people already seen their double faces.

They rush to interfere, when the friction is about another background. We often see 2 camps when strife breaks out, those of stakes and those for the right cause. Several young people haint respect towards their parents. A harmful behavior, they misbehave all the time. They insult, they mistreat their parents emotionally. They don't know the virtues and the importance of family. How someone can insult his parents? Or trying to rule at home? Responsibility of parents and some enforced laws are pointed. The system gave children a powerful stance, so don't be terrified to see them become hoodlums someday.

Children born through a system without definite rules, the system shapes their mentality then warns parents bout possible troubles if the children complain to social workers. The system prevents parents to educate correctly their children. They really fear to frustrate the adolescents, till you can see them negotiate with them. Parents are sacred, when you get stranded then facing your lot, that's too late, your chance has staled.

We can depose that we have the chance to yammer and to have the pick to accept or do not accept certain things of life. It seems when we have been fathered several things were affordable for us, gotta perceive it as a blessing of disguise. A chance that some kiddies through the world haint, cuz living in war zones or they have been begotten by base men, then face quandaries. We often can't feel kinda stress that some children are victim, if we don't experience it from top to bottom.

It seems only the mutilated can really utter about it, suffering that they daily meet, if they have the force put it into words. The third world countries already met the effect and can define the chaotic reality and its complexity. When you get kinda file in your palm's hands, you will perceive your chance, a sentiment that God spares you from something that you can't bring into words. And an occasion to be the eyewitness between the gap of the modern world and this world that nobody can give a real name. They already know about it, but behave as if the world was cleaned from kinda demons.

We all witness there are several worlds in a world, so how to repine when you are seeing countless cruel pics of starving children? Rare are people who enounce about it, as if everyone wants turning a blind eye; the subject stinks. Everybody is kvetching that the life is vederant, and shows themselves as sufferer of the system everywhere they step. They always lecture bearable topics or some other follies. But kinda turkeys never come across their minds, for most of em and prefer taking issue in other matters. We come to unravel when you suffer; there are other persons as you who find themselves in another level of suffering which haven't definition.

Most of us background openings that they have, and prefer propelling themselves in some far-out histories tied with suspicious activities, till find the hell underway. We can live quietly, if peeps were respectful, and then would the happiness for everybody. They have forbidden abortion, a normal finality, but a pregnancy conceals myriad realities. Numerous women continue to make abortion, in hiding.

Often these women assured that they loved their guys, but when arrive the moment to face responsibility the involved man jumps to it, first reality. A woman carries a baby and revealed the baby gets his origin from a rape, second reality. A woman can knowingly aborted, cuz she doesn't get what she expected on the man, third reality. These 3 are among other realities, anyway we can suppose if we fallowed what God already told, I think you will be not in kinda troubles. Some men act of kind; fathered children and not recognize them.

Of unsound mind these dudes are, they are often on the dole, no maturity of mind then they knock these wenches up. Kinda women are not prepared to be mom, and are in the dark about domesticity. You only have to see how they behave to understand that sentence. Exceeded by this dilemma, often the man asks to this woman to abort. The love wasn't the goal of their relation, but sex history that hid interests. Often some women try to face the difficulties and unbearable realities, a child with no visible father.

Unbearable situation, the mother has no means then counts on allowances. No able coping with, the man refuses the paternity. If the woman refuses to obey, the fatherhood can lead the man to disburse alimony. They ready to dissuade em, and they threat do not mind about baby. Under the strain they decide aborting for 2 grounds. Without aid from the man, they will have no means to feed the baby. The twice purpose is the reaction of parents, that numerous lasses had fear, when they got themselves up the pole before join in wedlock. Most of women gave birth anonymously to avoid critics.

But our era has changed tendencies, cuz nowadays a baby who came from criminal conversation is nothing, and that became a success and a happy event, just to have baby count for most of em. Parents are so happy to be granddad in all conditions, it's why deceptions multiplied. Before the alarm was justified, because often some parents don't admit the fornication.

They often expel their daughter from house then tell her to cope, without get ulterior motive, what she will be once in genus Ruta with her pregnancy. Those who aborted present after effects, and are submersed by rues. We can call them criminal, cuz it's a criminal act. Imagine your mother had kinda initiative during you been a foetus, are you will be here today to make a similar deed?

We can name you felon, if the act does not linked with indecent assault; you had knowingly assented to hook up. If linked with rape you will be alone having it on your slate, but an actus Reus remains an evildoing. Some individuals span yarns that the abortion creates 2 dead. I amn't convinced, in most of case there is one dead. The society backs the legal requested abortion and obscured the criminal act behind, they are pro-choice. Most persons became haggling, their conception is devoid of meaning then spreads dangerously the hair brain ideas most of time. Kinda wenches dehumanized themselves unconsciously, and sometimes knowingly.

Kinda persons are surrounded by insincere persons who don't itemize to them, the detriment of this human activity. They got their girlfriends up the spout without know about, cuz the wench miscarried on the quiet. You ain't having the chance do not agnise that your dame wasn't hazen toward you. Since most body politics turn it as modus- operandi, the abortion reaches record high rates. At the other side certain countries strictly forbade this criminal act in their respective land, if it does not imply sexual assault, or if the mother faces complications, with threat of penalties. What about certain res publica which is prey to abortion often performed abortion under duress, we can witness.

They go till make selective abortion; it appears that the world is held by several acts of faith. We also witness some countries strongly hold back "termination of pregnancy" whatever the cause of this pregnancy in some lands. So mind where you step before to challenge procedures, if you ain't wanna troubles, cuz this will be not handle-able.

The doings of some persons are all kinds of agnorant, mixed with a vacuous oral character that can make you feel a head lock. Most of em vache in town nooks then gaze at different persons either over the moon persons or with insipidity. All scenarios in streets been noticed, those who scoop cigarette butt without be embarrassed by the look of peeps. They don't care; they are living another time, where they are not crunched a while, but anytime. Walking up to passers-by is most of em ploy; just hoping gotta cigarette leftover or insignificant things.

Ascertained that numerous wage earners deport themselves as dossers, aiming to get something on pass as, begging clams, and some stuff just to allay the daily disorders they are daily facing. 'Bout their carriage, they don't mind, even some looks definite them as street person. Another category of citizens your eyes can scan discriminatory, cuz they embody the scenery of misery. No far are standing the neutral spirit sympathizers. Not cognizant when they are between ganja and neutral spirit, hard is the life they are leading.

Truculent, jumbled they are when these 3 are about to drone their minds, until be zonked, whilst pigs are doing rounds to preclude scuffles. Often brawls break out when they are half-cut, or high, cuz they become jumbled. The neutral spirits became the best companion of nowadays people; the social status does not matter. Most of time impels em in police custody, that's shamuses really like just to get busy a while. I ain't averring they are waiting their time turn in better life. Rather it seems they are waiting unconsciously a plight for next years. Plights linked for next coming contentions that those who have something to lose in troubles have feared.

The villains are watching it carefully, and someday to flee will be the only option. They wondering where were hiding these villains? They hide themselves nowhere; they just are the aimless citizens that you always underestimate in the daily life. Aimless citizens that leaders encourage in the way of hate and mediocrity, staring the society's system consumes em step by step.

To abscond will be the only option, I 'amn't sure, cuz everywhere got affected. Involved or not involved, it seems everyone will have a share of the pie. They all often clustered in some areas of town as if it was a jamboree, a foregathering that happens every day as if they haint a vocation. Through kinda throng is standing all type of individuals. Trim persons who seem to be bored stiff in their tenement are perceived there. You also can eye hombres or dolls highlighting their know-how to make a lucrative meeting.

"Lucrative" according their frame of mind; they are looking for kindred spirit, or to come across a poor fish to gouge. Life throws em a dare that driving all em crazy, a new craze they strive to oust negatively. No public-spiritedness your eyes can scan. They going for a leak, they spit or spill over the booze bad smell in all over the place, public transportation not spared so. A key idem that we all together have to overcome with sitzfleish, even we already twig this will be not quite a job.

A crazy bearing, nonsense talks as if they were in another dimension, whilst the air is pervade by invisible substances or dark smokes that outing from several mouths. That dark smoke became a scent for their noses and a horror for the non-smokers. The air seems being not pure anymore, flooded by kinda toxic substances. Cancerogenic substances they happily drive into their sad lungs. Lots of illnesses have been occasioned by their lack of esteem toward others and towards their self-integrity.

Only the present pleasure can touch their sensibility, and egg em on to enjoy full of it, without care those who standing beside them are getting affected. "Got hunch in world streets most of people became wacky, performing nonsense gestures and talks. Don't be bewildered by what Weltschmerz may engender as personal manner, cuz already notified us we live in idiocracy. Looniest people ain't all dwelling in loony bin, but are ambulating in world streets.

Kinda situations can usher in hecticity, till in some countries you can eyeball some bulls forgathered, and policing around strategic areas. On the lookout they are; a deportment against suspicious moves, an angle fed by the growth of ruffianism. This deposes everyone's slant of life; and 'bout some happenings the deteriorating of chivalry. Riots of hungry are again her, booming, in front of this plight non force, non-organization can kibosh the wind that are the despair of. Kinda disorders sire violent fisticuffs that often turn out in mortal combat.

Several people brought into the open that life wipes em out. This statement will always sound sham till the day they all immune from blame. Only humans tear down the world then cry behind. They were assessing that hungry riots were belonged to old ages, or certain zones of the planet. But the future has proven we were in the right, cuz the manner they would that the world works, launched the world into a critical situation. It re-emerges where most of people don't ideate found it. They had a cow and didn't interested by what taking place in the rest of the world.

Assessed wrongly, they were thinking to be spared, forgetting that their own world was found on earth. Making strong credit and gage em as geni ==their leaders. And today they complain what the hell's wrong with em, it seems they fall em short. Bordering on rage, kinda populace haint ider and began tossing toward em first vituperations. The phenomenon is in the offing, nowadays they all talk bout the subject, whilst some people were in kinda kettle of fish for donkey years. What were you doing whilst they were steeling to brave the gant, and bemoan their lot?

You were only basking your chance on em. Cuz you always had a savory steak on your plate and what are repelling you today? You're cornered and licked that each era will be a bygone days. We shoulda contend against that depression during the situation was going through veter. In lieu of interact they turned a blind eye. Turn a blind eye then gotten foregone upshots. They wanted to vark, but Gordian knot comes to them. Hard to mend and being victims, the plight roused em; they are in the doldrums and seem going off the rails.

Have anymore a Hac, and can't expose their condescension. Their voices sound despicable, notified us 2 losses 'bout them (their babbitry and Harvey). 'Alighted the world streets, giving testimony in front of cameras, bring into light their financial crunch as chronicle. They squirm them money in the futility, cuz already realized their allure from worldly, then are making riches on their amentia. More they produce, more they buy sans picture the dark coming days that everybody will face whether he wanna yes or no. It will strike soon and you will take your responsibility, in the manner it will appear at your side.

They know what the secularism may engender as troubles in the long run, but don't alert them to prevent the consequences. They often see someone else's misfortune, till it strikes home. Kinda phenomenon has taken shape hazardously and continues throwing its worldwide effects. This new era results from philistinism, several individuals linked happiness with materialism. Sole a stupid can colligate these 2 in all aspects.

The cult of materialism ain't necessarily installed a long term happiness and success in people's life. Even there are people who strive to substantiate the contrary everywhere they go. You only can influence those who are as thick as two planks, but not us who cling on credence that laid in the positive moral excellence. In the past it was a mistake to believe that having possessions will turn your life happy. But nowadays that's a positive trend, and will make you popular whatever your state of mind and your origins. You will be welcomed with best conditions.

They don't try cajoling people that everything is material, that's an archaic task; cuz the people already joined their materialist mentality. It seems that nowadays people born materialist and transmit this bad belief to their circle of acquaintances. They all shout out that they don't like the materialists, but they also are materialists by their state of mind. They only told that because they are fear to be cheated by their compatriots, who have same desires as em.

And also they don't like that the non-materialists turn aside, when they met them in the Ruta. Terrible short-comings and seem being intractable, unavowable suffering when you couple with kinda persons. You can feel the hyper when you designate em as materialists, rejecting fiercely what they really are. Even you deny we can feel your negative pulchritude everywhere you go. Some people told the materialists are less jolly than the non-materialists. I don't know but one thing I am sure they deteriorated mores, everywhere they pass with their dark mental makeup.

They have no moral decency cuz poverty spreads. In kinda behavior sole the non-concerned are victims of kinda predators. You can perceive some comportment that you can't give a real sense. You will only cotton on this came from the dark side, they become inane and blind, whilst the world is launching to extinction. They wanna succeed swiftly in these troubles, launching in the quest of success, without really know what is the success and its contents.

Hazardous to gonna toward a conquest road that you can define the signs, and hid histories behind. When you questioned most of em why they wanna having achievement, the retort is shattering. I am persuading that the materialism can't be mixed with religion, cuz these 2 go through different ways. Either you are with God or you belonged to another clan (dark side).So they all are greedy till they all forgotten the sense of life, and the meaning of their coming hither. Their strong belief dictates em to situate God in the background, but the wise human has pity about kinda souls who seem already lost in the dark.

Lost for certain people who seem sink forever, and only make in application human volitions. Behaving as predators to reach opulence, even they can't afford; a suffering that emanates from moral conflict. The profusion they all wanna, lack of virtues they ain't care. Your desire of material will drive you to ruin, in all aspects later. Through this quest you are a blind (in the kingdom of blind the one eyed man is king).

The tempter already won the combat in worldly, but will lose it in a well-defined time, lose it the day this scheduled occurrence will happen. Not hemmed in by what surrounding em, some people launch themselves into idiotic speculations. Affright of apocalypse is turning into extravaganza, clan movements your eyes can severalize, whilst phenomenon upping hazardously. Apocalyptic discourses escalating every day and are far and near. Apocalyptic addresses began cutting a dash on the dumbest minds, till turn in faction. Chesty, acquisitive they are to prophesy the end of time, as if it was them who coined the world then sent predilections.

You're feckless to emboss suitably your life and to foreshadow your fate in the ten next minutes, why coming bug our minds with a close at hand Armageddon? There are cited burghs as sacred and spared lands during the apocalypse day. Scheduled apocalypse tied with goal, which is nothing other than the mazuma. They are profiting from this fright and on people simple-mindedness.

The merchants of fear are accruing since they make out the stake of that Irish bull. They passed from charlatan status toward guru status, having on every aficionado a psychological expropriation, just to worm their gelt till the last coin; "the earth will be your nirvana". I was thought that the dedicated films on apocalypse were cine-films as others, but we were barking up the wrong tree, cuz it turned people as barking mad. Affective Psychosis is snowballing and people are no more compos mentis. The motion picture has a spooky impact. They are about to echo same gestures and state of mind that emerged from the motion picture. A no productive mind will envisage that the end of time will emerged from scientific speculations, and there will have survivals.

Only a receptive mind will conceptualize that the end of time will occurs from the divine aspect. The democracy is a positive get up and go, but can drive into lunacy according everyone standpoint. We only can be a disparager, when we look their state of mind. Not knowing where kinda fiction took shape until leads people through an absolute sanity.

In their quest to two-time the feeble-minded you can sense a demoniacal perversity, when they about to bring them into amentia. A lese-majesty and disbelief toward God, your eyes can notice it, full of suspense. They excogitated in the end of time there will have subsister. We agreeing but you better give his holy name. Look them blundering about, spending rhino as hair brained to have farcical survival training.

Moneyed citizens who are in the heazy buy a sand trap as hideout to get away from apocalypse, mulling in the apocalypse, the cataclysm will remains on earth's surface. You all need to open or to reopen the lexicon to larn in a deep learning about words meanings. Whilst other buffs of the clan have chosen the most frenzied way, gonzo for our minds, but sacred and holy for their minds. Some among them planned to clamber on a cliff's top and fall from there. They have a strong belief that heaven's gates will open yonder then give to them a jiffy to intrude into the put-on breach.

Some people voiced that these talks are grisly grapevines, whilst most ultra-spirits turn these pipelines as garbage. You really need schooling yourselves and brush away these notional occurrences, and take the line that leads you to learn signs. Hellish cults are a social phenomenon, gaining ground in wide-world then enticed several people to launch into fiendish beliefs. Numerous they are to rejoin the parallel world. This first step to adhere in kinda sect becomes run of the mill.

An eery opening move linked with touch-and-go emerging denominations. The society is revering the fiend then undergoes a negative transference. Some of em are amiss 'bout their coming here, then ain't realize the negative mutation that they are engendering in every aspect. This nescience does not the same history of some persons who already know the line they are taking then adhere to become powerful. They already aired a message to controvert 'bout the divine say-so.

None compliance and faith toward God, who looks em misbehave, God doesn't hurry to point em out the right way radically. The devil represents the success for em. The devil embodies the great mare's nest in this era, and throws people in constant mutation. The demon cult became a strength organization; the initiation is based by stage and rituals. The Old-nick is getting stronger in this dirt modern world, all that agitation is nothing than a vulgar dust; insignificant dust that God will brushs away at the appropriate time.

All that mess have been mentioned for years, God doesn't tremble and he will never tremble. God has not time for kinda disorders. Despite all these noises, comings and goings Satan already knows the line that he must not trespass; and the undisputed supremacy of the Supreme-being. That sentence is a reality that the human being snubs by lack of deep study. Several humans being are ignoramus, cuz they got a devil may-care attitude. Satan is the master of the worldly, but not the master of the world.

The world is sourced of materialist people; and several persons are under his orders by lucrative needs. Most of em became vulgar daemons here on earth, when they wheel and deal in hiding with the fallen angel (all that in God's eyes). Some people who reverence the demon's cult use waving to commune unobtrusively, "There are no flies on us". The Satanism-already led in profanations, and ritual murders and myriad dirties acts.

Several lives have been sacrificed for blasphemous causes. Before anybody's eyes some worshippers make demoniacal ceremonies, during adepts seem rhapsodic. Some disciples of the Satanism ain't identifiable, cuz they leading a normal life before peeps' eyes. The cult of Satanism is the dreamed way for those who wanna fully live the forbidden desires in the abysmal world. "I sold my soul to devil, I became stronger, you can feel kinda mien in their comportment and in their daily life". But in our side we venerate the Supreme-being; he gave us breath and made us what we are today.

Thank him every day to have given us sensitive spirits for the discernment. Satan never gives something in the long run. Satan only learns receiving but does not give favourable things. The horror in all its bearings pervaded our era till extreme excitations, what remain to us to discover? The tempters are diffusing their demonic cult everywhere (music, films, conferences, violent video games etc. Consider as exploit the time that you devote to God every day in worldly. Very hard is to venerate Him trough worldly, when you see how Satan turned it in huge mess. Satan is an efficient soul stealer.

The Satanism is the only dark belief that encourages people to evidence their individual desires every day and everywhere. They are trying to fight down a creator God idea, they only have a firebrand spirit, "but this cuts no ice with us". A state of mind which is conflicting with our culture and belief, it's why we pooh-pooh it by all odds.

Those who are leading Satanism sect are only reproducing the plan of the authentic religion a contrario. Several leaders of Satanism are dead in knowing the power and the profusion all their life. To believe is a dimness sign and incapacity to manage his life according their state of mind. They only wanna that the falsehood and the lack of confidence toward God spread. Even if the Tempter is joined by several lost souls every day, there are few remaining persons who are struggling against his enterprise. The followers of Satan are at the image of their master.

The Satanism is a sect of rebellion which is based on hopeless theories. They only venerate Satan–to have the horn of plenty, a favor that always remains in worldly. They only got the status symbol that does not lure the god fearing men. Satan is only seeking companions for the furnace. This will be very terrifying day, when the verity breaks out. Horrendous day when all Satan's shits will are in the furnace. You will be in deep waters, if you step in god's kingdom with empty hands.

© 2015 - Papa Seyni Faye
Edition: BoD - Books on Demand
12/14 rond-point des Champs Elysées, 75008 Paris
Imprimé par Books on Demand GmbH, Norderstedt, Allemagne
ISBN : 9782322042623
Dépôt légal: novembre 2015